W9-BZA-153

# CONTENTS

**1 YOUR MONEY PROFILE** ..... 1

**2 YOUR SOURCES OF RETIREMENT INCOME** ..... 7
The Different Types of Retirement Plans ..... 7
Other Sources of Retirement Income ..... 11

**3 HOW MUCH MONEY WILL YOU NEED TO RETIRE?** ..... 14
Working Through the Numbers ..... 14
Are You Saving Enough for Retirement? ..... 16

**4 LEARNING THE BASICS OF SAVING AND INVESTING** ..... 21
Safe Investments Versus Risky Ones ..... 21
How Bonds Work ..... 23
How CDs Work ..... 26
How Money Market Accounts Work ..... 26

**5 THE BASICS OF INVESTING IN STOCKS** ..... 28
What Are Stocks? ..... 28
How to Buy Stocks ..... 31
Where to Learn More About a Particular Stock ..... 33

**6 THE WONDER OF MUTUAL FUNDS** ..... 35
The Basics of Mutual Funds ..... 35
What's a Mutual Fund? ..... 35
Choosing the Right Funds ..... 36
Where to Buy Mutual Funds ..... 40

**7 TAKING ADVANTAGE OF TAX-DEFERRED ANNUITIES** ..... 41
What Is an Annuity? ..... 41
Evaluating the Types of Annuities ..... 44
Withdrawing the Funds ..... 44

**8 INVESTING IN GUARANTEED INVESTMENT CONTRACTS AND EMPLOYEE STOCK OWNERSHIP PLANS** ..... 46
Investing in Guaranteed Investment Contracts (GICs) ..... 46
Investing in Employee Stock Ownership Plans (ESOPs) ..... 49

**9 BECOMING A RISK TAKER** ..... 51
Getting Started as a Risk Taker ..... 51
Start Small ..... 51
Saving on Commissions ..... 52
Educate Yourself ..... 54
Join an Investment Club ..... 54

**10    Putting Together Your Portfolio    56**

Balancing Your Portfolio .................................................. 56
The Importance of Rebalancing .............................................. 58
The Magic of Regular Savings ............................................ 59

**11    How Changing Jobs Impacts Your Retirement    61**

Why Job-Jumping Can Hurt Your Retirement Savings ......... 61
The Trouble with Taking Time Off from the Workplace ...... 63
The Financial Implications ...................................... 64

**12    Marriage, Divorce, and Retirement Planning    66**

Plan to Be Alone ........................................................ 66
What You Can Do Now ................................................. 67
Consider a Prenuptial Agreement .................................... 68
Take Action Before You Divorce ................................... 68
What Your QDRO Must Contain ................................. 70
Time Your Divorce .................................................... 70

**13    The Toll of Medical Expenses    71**

Health Care for Seniors ........................................... 71
Taking Advantage of Medicare ...................................... 71
Medicare Supplement Policies ..................................... 73
Finding Out More About Medicare and Medigap Policies .... 74
Long-Term Care Insurance ...................................... 74
What Long-Term Care Policies Cover ......................... 75
What Does Long-Term Insurance Cost? .......................... 76
Finding a Policy ..................................................... 76
What to Look for in a Policy .................................... 76
How to Trim Premium Costs ..................................... 78

**14    Working Beyond Retirement    79**

What to Make of an Early Retirement Offer ..................... 79
The Case for Working After Retirement ....................... 80
Delay Applying for Social Security ............................ 81
Partial Retirement ................................................. 82
How to Find Part-Time Work ................................... 83
Starting Your Own Business ..................................... 83
Working and Social Security .................................... 84

**15    Tapping Into Your Home Equity    85**

Home Equity Lines of Credit .................................... 85
Reverse Mortgages ................................................. 86
Other Housing Alternatives ..................................... 89
Staying Put .......................................................... 90

**16 Looking Into Life and Disability Insurance** — **91**

Life Insurance as a Retirement Tool ....................................... 91
Calculating the Amount of Life Insurance You Need ........... 93
What Kind of Insurance Should You Buy? ............................ 93
Who Should Consider a Cash-Value Policy? ........................ 95
Withdrawing the Money ....................................................... 95
Shopping for Term Insurance ............................................... 96
Tracking Down the Best Price on a Policy ........................... 97
Shopping for Cash-Value Policies ........................................ 97
Don't Ignore Disability Insurance ........................................ 98
Cost-Saving Tips .................................................................. 99

**17 Estate Planning and Trusts** — **100**

The Living Trust .................................................................. 100
How to Pick a Trustee ......................................................... 103
How to Execute a Trust ....................................................... 103

**18 Estate Planning and Gifts** — **104**

Educational Gifts and Medical Gifts ................................... 104
Charitable Gifts .................................................................. 105
Charitable Remainder Trusts .............................................. 106
How a Charitable Gift Annuity Works ................................ 107

**19 Choosing a Financial Planner** — **108**

Can You Do It Yourself? ..................................................... 108
How to Choose a Planner .................................................... 109
Finding a Planner ............................................................... 110
What You Should Ask a Planner .......................................... 111
What a Planner Should Ask You .......................................... 112

**20 Going On-Line For Help** — **114**

On-Line Services ................................................................ 114
Investment Forums ............................................................. 115
America Online ................................................................... 115
CompuServe ....................................................................... 116
Prodigy .............................................................................. 117
The Internet's World Wide Web ......................................... 117
Where to Start .................................................................... 118
Other Useful Sites .............................................................. 118

**A Resources** — **120**

**B Glossary** — **123**

**Index** — **130**

# INTRODUCTION

Retirement planning is a serious issue for everyone. And the likelihood that you'll live 20 years or more in retirement makes it even more so. As a woman, preparing for your retirement is perhaps the most critical financial challenge you face. Consider this:

- Women earn less than men—roughly 72 cents for every dollar a man earns—so the funds that can be set aside for retirement are more scarce.

- Women are more likely to work for smaller firms that have no pension plan at all, or in jobs such as real estate sales that have meager pension offerings at best.

- Reduced salaries mean smaller Social Security payouts and slimmer pension benefits, too.

- The average woman retiring today at age 65 is expected to live another 20 years, and life expectancies are increasing.

- Women live, on average, seven years longer than men, so they need more funds set aside to protect against outliving their income.

- Many women take time off from work to raise a family or care for an aging relative. The result: fewer years they can pay into a retirement plan.

- Women tend to invest their money conservatively. As a result, even when they do save for retirement, their returns are far below what they might be if they took more risks with the types of investments they pick.

Whether you are 20 or 50, there are some important retirement planning lessons that will help you combat the financial dilemma you may well face when you retire. Your retirement planning game plan will depend on several factors, including your current age, the number of years until you retire, the pool of money you have to invest, how willing you are to take some risks with your investments, and any other income sources or assets such as your home that will add a significant sum of money to your retirement chest.

The *10 Minute Guide to Retirement for Women* has information
that every woman needs to learn: the basics of building and
protecting a nest egg for a headache-free retirement. It teaches
you the basics of retirement planning in a series of short lessons that can be completed in 10 minutes or less. Because each
lesson is self-contained, you can start and stop as time permits.
This and other aspects of the *10 Minute Guide to Retirement for
Women* make it perfect for anyone who:

- Has a restricted amount of time to spend planning
  for their retirement.
- Is intimidated by the concepts of investing and
  saving.
- Wants an easy-to-understand guide to the essential
  elements of planning for a financially secure future.
- Needs to determine today if they are saving enough
  to retire comfortably.

# WHAT IS THE 10 MINUTE GUIDE?

The 10 Minute Guide series is a new approach to learning the
basics of investing. Instead of trying to teach you every aspect
of retirement financial planning, the 10 Minute Guide teaches
you just those aspects that are essential.

This 10 Minute Guide will teach you about investing and saving without relying on financial jargon. You'll only find plain
English in this book to explain the steps of planning for retirement. With straightforward, easy-to-follow steps and special
icons to call your attention to important tips and definitions,
the 10 Minute Guide makes learning how to manage your
retirement plan fast and easy.

# CONVENTIONS USED IN THIS BOOK

The following icons help you find your way around the *10
Minute Guide to Retirement for Women*:

**tip** Tips offer shortcuts and hints for planning for retirement.

Plain English icons identify definitions of new terms.

Panic Button icons appear in places where new investors often run into trouble.

The *10 Minute Guide to Retirement for Women* contains 20 lessons. Most readers will want to work through the lessons in that order. After reading the first three lessons, however, you can jump around if you need specific information quickly.

It's never too late to save for retirement. The odds are good that you will be entirely responsible for your own financial well-being at some point in your life. By saving and planning for your own retirement, you will be assured of financial freedom, regardless of what life throws at you.

## ACKNOWLEDGEMENTS

The following is a list of the people and organizations who helped me understand the need for women to plan for their retirement with wisdom and confidence. They made this guide possible.

Alexandra Armstrong, financial planner, Washington, D.C.; Esther M. Berger, PaineWebber, Inc., Beverly Hills; Ann B. Diamond, financial consultant, New York City; Victoria Felton-Collins, author; Karen Ferguson, Pension Rights Center; Claire Friedrichs, Smith Barney, New Orleans; Diane Harris, *Working Woman* magazine; The National Center for Women and Retirement Research; Martha Priddy Patterson, KMPG Peat Marwick, Washington, D.C.; Judy Resnick, Dabney/Resnick, Beverly Hills; Carolyn Stolz, American Express, New Orleans.

Thanks also to Patricia H. Bonney, Becky Hackel, Clifford Hackel, John W. Hannon, and Marguerite Hannon.

# YOUR MONEY PROFILE

*In this lesson, you'll learn how to build the foundation of your retirement plan by answering some critical questions about your own financial makeup.*

To lay the groundwork for a comfortable and financially solid retirement, you must start by taking a hard look at your unique situation. It's possible to satisfy your desire to retire with a fat nest egg. You have the ability to save enough money to keep you living in style for another 20 years or so, after you step out of the workforce. To make that goal a reality, you'll need to get started now. The sooner you start, the easier it will be to meet your goals.

If you think that living in retirement will be much less expensive than how you're living now, you're fooling yourself. It's true that you won't have the upkeep of a work wardrobe or the expenses of commuting, or maybe even the cost of $10 lunches each day. But in the end, those savings aren't as significant as you might imagine. And other costs, such as travel expenses, may well go up. In general, you will need 80 percent of your preretirement income annually to continue to live in the same fashion after you retire. Tightwads might be able to squeeze by on 70 percent, but it's best to plan for the higher figure.

Of course, that's 80 percent of your annual income at retirement. To estimate that, you'll need to get a grip on how inflation takes a toll on both your income and your savings. Inflation has averaged 3.1 percent a year for the last 70 years. What that means is that something that costs $1,000 now will jump to $1,300 in 10 years and $1,600 in 20 years. Meantime, your salary, say $40,000 today, might rise to $52,000 in a decade, providing your employer keeps it in line with inflation. To be on the safe side, for your planning purposes, estimate that inflation will rise 4 percent a year between now and the year you retire. Then expect, if all goes well, that your salary will increase 3 percent annually over inflation for a total increase of 7 percent a year.

To accumulate enough money to match 80 percent of your preretirement income, your investments as well as your salary will need to outpace inflation. That 3.1 percent inflation gain can quickly eat away investment gains. That's why it's crucial you put your retirement savings in investment vehicles that solidly beat inflation year in and year out. As you'll learn in later lessons, many investments that savers *think* are safe spots to stash their retirement are, in fact, too conservative and over the long haul don't beat the inflation rate. Some of these are certificates of deposit, bonds, and money market accounts.

Now that you have a rough estimate of what your target retirement money needs might be, consider what other factors may influence your retirement financial scenario. Take out a notebook and jot down the answers to the following financial questions. Your responses will help you determine what your money needs will be when you retire:

- What's your money philosophy? Do you tend to be a frugal saver or do you spend money as fast as you make it?

- Do you expect to inherit money one day? If so, how much is it likely to be, and how many years from now might you get the money?

- Is your current job secure? This is a tough question to answer in these days of corporate downsizing, but give it some serious thought.

- What are your prospects for raises and promotions?

- Do you have children to educate?

- Are you sending children through college?

- Do you still have a house mortgage or home equity loan?

- Do you expect to support your spouse one day?

- Do you expect to support your parents or in-laws one day?

- What are your financial goals for retirement? For instance, do you want to have enough money to travel around the world?

- What kind of lifestyle do you envision?

- Do you have any medical conditions that will require expensive care?

- Do you have any children who will remain dependent on you because of health reasons?

- Will you have a house to sell at a gain when you retire?

- Do you have a small business you might sell at retirement?

Your answers to these questions will dramatically impact your retirement. No two people will have the same set of circumstances to work with. A woman who wants to travel extensively in those golden years will need to save far more than someone who has no taste for globetrotting. Someone who has a house to sell at retirement has a lump sum to tap into that a person who rents doesn't. And so on.

Now that you have a feel for what your future needs might be, take a snapshot of where your present income comes from, where it goes, and your current living expenses by jotting them down on the Current Assets/Liabilities worksheet on the following page.

**Assets and Liabilities**  Assets are everything that you own—your house, a diamond ring, your car. Liabilities are everything that you owe—credit card debt, mortgage, student loans.

**Expenses and Income**  Expenses are what you spend each month. That usually means your rent or mortgage payment, car payment and insurance, telephone, electric and gas bills, as well as food and transportation costs. Income is your salary or other money you receive for full-time, part-time, or freelance work. Income also includes any money that you receive from investments, such as a house that you rent to others or interest from savings accounts and dividends paid by stocks or mutual funds.

Figuring out how much you spend each year and how much you bring in will help you find ways to save those extra funds for your retirement.

### CURRENT ASSETS/LIABILITIES WORKSHEET

#### WHAT ARE YOU WORTH TODAY?

##### ASSETS

Your current annual income: $_____

Checking account balance: $_____

Savings account: $_____

Certificates of deposit: $_____

Savings bonds: $_____

What your home is worth: $_____

Value of any other property you own: $_____

Cash value of life insurance policies: $_____

Value of your pension or profit-sharing stake:  $_____

IRA and Keogh plans: $_____

Current value of any stocks you own: $_____

Current value of any bonds you hold: $_____

Current value of any mutual funds you own: $_____

Market value of any other investments: $_____

Value of your car(s): $_____

Value of your furniture: $_____

Value of your clothing and jewelry: $_____

Total assets: $_____

*continues*

## CURRENT ASSETS/LIABILITIES WORKSHEET

### WHAT ARE YOU WORTH TODAY?

#### EXPENSES

Mortgage balance or rent due on existing lease: $_____

Credit card balances:  $_____

Auto loan or total lease payments due: $_____

Outstanding student loans:  $_____

Annual auto insurance payments:  $_____

Annual health insurance payments:  $_____

Annual home or renters insurance payments: $_____

Annual property taxes:  $_____

Annual utility bills:  $_____

Estimated yearly clothing expenses:  $_____

Estimated annual travel expenses:  $_____

Estimated annual transportation expenses (gas, parking, auto repairs): $_____

Total liabilities:  $_____

In this lesson, you built the foundation of your retirement plan by answering some important questions about your personal finances and future spending demands. In the next lesson, you'll learn what your sources of retirement income are likely to be.

# YOUR SOURCES OF RETIREMENT INCOME

*In this lesson, you'll learn what sources of retirement income are available and how you can take advantage of them.*

## THE DIFFERENT TYPES OF RETIREMENT PLANS

Creating a retirement plan is like stitching together a quilt. No two patterns are exactly alike because each person has different sources of funds, varying levels of income, and will retire at different ages. For instance, the amount you will receive from the government in the form of Social Security will vary widely depending on your earnings and how much time you spent in the workforce. Some employers provide traditional pensions. With other employers, you must decide how much of your salary you want to set aside in tax-deferred accounts and in what types of investments you want your employer to invest for you.

If you're self-employed, you'll need to set up your own tax-deferred plan.

Here are three elements of retirement income you will need in order to live comfortably:

- An employer-provided plan
- Social Security
- Your own savings and investments

 **Your own savings**   The only element under your complete control is your own savings. On average, over half of your retirement income will need to come from your wages, personal savings, and investments.

This list from the Social Security Administration shows where your retirement income will come from:

Investments: 34%

Your wages: 24%

Social Security: 21%

Pensions: 19%

Other: 2%

Here are the basic retirement plans offered by employers:

- *Defined benefit plan.* A defined benefit plan is a traditional pension plan in which your employer devises a formula, based on your salary and the number of years you've worked with the company, to calculate income that will be paid to you when you retire. When you retire, the money is paid out to you on a monthly basis for the rest of your life.

- *Defined contribution plan.* A defined contribution plan is one in which your employer contributes a set amount for you annually in a retirement fund. When you retire, you are usually paid the accumulated funds in a lump sum.

  A 401(k) plan is a popular type of defined contribution retirement plan. With a 401(k), you set aside a portion of your salary into mutual funds or other investment choices. You avoid paying any taxes on that portion of your salary, or on the earnings that accumulate, until you withdraw the money. Most employers contribute some amount to the plan, often on a partially matching basis after you've worked for a certain number of years. This is called a vesting period and is usually around five years. The annual limit on pre-tax 401(k) contributions for 1996 is $9,500. A 403(b) plan is similar to a 401(k) for public employees and employees of non-profit organizations.

- *Employee Stock Ownership Plan (ESOP).* An ESOP is a retirement plan in which your employer makes contributions in the form of the company's stock.

**tip** To find out more about how pension plans work, call the U.S. Department of Labor at (202) 219-8776, or write Pension and Welfare Benefits Administration, Washington, D.C. 20210 and request a free booklet called "What You Should Know About Your Pension Rights."

If you're a woman without an employer-sponsored plan, there are still several ways you can put aside tax-deferred retirement income:

- *Individual Retirement Account (IRA).* All working women are eligible to contribute as much as $2,000 a year to an Individual Retirement Account, or IRA. All or part of the contribution is tax-deductible and any interest earned accumulates tax-free until the funds are withdrawn when you are 59 1/2 or older. Early withdrawals are usually slapped with a 10 percent penalty by the Internal Revenue Service (unless you can prove economic hardship), and the money is taxed as income for the year. You must, however, begin withdrawing the money by the time you are 70 1/2. An IRA can be invested in certificates of deposit, bonds, mutual funds, or stocks, among other options. There are a few restrictions, though. For example, investing in gold is prohibited. An IRA is especially critical if you work for a company that does not offer a pension plan.

- *Keogh plan.* Similar to an IRA, a Keogh is a good way to save for retirement, particularly if you are temporarily off the payroll but still have a few consulting or freelance projects. If you are self-employed, a freelancer, or have your own business, you can set up a tax-deductible Keogh plan. As much as 20 percent of self-employment income can be put in a Keogh. Earnings are tax-deferred until you withdraw them at age 59 1/2, or at retirement.

- *Simplified Employee Pension Plan (SEP).* You can set up a SEP for yourself that allows you to deduct roughly 15 percent of your self-employed net earnings. The money accumulated is tax-free until you retire.

**tip**  After you know what types of plans are available to you, start a file for all your pension information, including your paycheck stubs.

# OTHER SOURCES OF RETIREMENT INCOME

Another important source of money for your retirement is Social Security benefits.

To qualify for Social Security benefits as a wage earner you must have 40 quarters of coverage. One quarter of coverage is granted for each $570 earned, so $2,280 a year comes to four quarters of coverage. You may qualify for Social Security benefits as the spouse of a wage earner, even if you are divorced. The rule is you must have been married for at least 10 years.

Under the current system, Social Security replaces about 42 percent of your pay if you earn average wages. If your earnings are lower, it replaces as much as 88 percent. If you have higher earnings, it replaces close to 25 percent of your salary that was subject to Social Security taxes.

The following table lists your estimated monthly Social Security benefits at retirement.

## APPROXIMATE MONTHLY SOCIAL SECURITY BENEFITS AT 65 (1990$)

| PRESENT AGE | BENEFITS RECIPIENT | YOUR EARNINGS | | | |
|---|---|---|---|---|---|
| | | $20,000 | $30,000 | $40,000 | $50,000 |
| 45 | You | $863 | $1,124 | $1,263 | $1,392 |
| | You/Spouse | $1,294 | $1,686 | $1,894 | $2,088 |
| 55 | You | $783 | $1,014 | $1,106 | $1,181 |
| | You/Spouse | $1,174 | $1,521 | $1,659 | $1,771 |
| 65 | You | $725 | $926 | $982 | $1,021 |
| | You/Spouse | $1,087 | $1,389 | $1,473 | $1,531 |

These figures will vary by your past and future earnings and assume you and your spouse are the same age.

*Source: Social Security Administration*

**tip**

**Keep track of your accrued benefits**   Every three years you should get a copy of your Earnings and Benefit Estimate Statement from the Social Security Administration. To get this information, call 800-772-1213. This will allow you to fix any errors that may appear and be certain that the Administration has accurate information about your wage history. Moreover, if you tell the Social Security Administration at what age you expect to retire, you can receive your estimated benefit at retirement. There is no charge for this information.

If you're fortunate enough to participate in a company sponsored retirement plan, it's your responsibility to read all the plan information to understand how the plan operates and any restrictions that apply to you. Bear in mind the following important points:

- Don't ignore a vesting period if one applies to your plan. According to the Bureau of Labor Statistics, women over 25 stay with an employer an average of 4.8 years (compared with 6.6 years for men)—just a few months shy of the five years typically required to fully qualify for a pension or an employer's contribution to a 401(k) plan.

- If you do jump jobs, be sure to transfer any plan payout you do receive from your former employer into another tax-deferred account, such as a rollover 401(k). It is advantageous to opt for a direct rollover to another tax-deferred account. By doing this, the plan administrator does not withhold tax from the distribution. This way your money can keep growing tax-deferred into a big chunk of change before retirement arrives.

- Don't be afraid to ask your firm's employee benefits office questions if there is something you don't understand.

- Get in the habit of reviewing your plan at least every six months.

In this lesson, you learned about your sources of retirement income and how the types of retirement savings work. In the next lesson, you'll learn to calculate how much money you will need to retire comfortably.

# How Much Money Will You Need to Retire?

*In this lesson, you'll learn to calculate how much money you need to save for retirement.*

## Working Through the Numbers

The precise sum of money you'll need to cover future living expenses is nearly impossible to calculate. But there are ways to estimate how much money you're likely to want to have on hand.

For this lesson, you'll need to have several important pieces of financial information, including your estimated Social Security payout at retirement and estimated employee pension at retirement. If you don't have the necessary numbers readily available to you, you may need to split this lesson into two sessions.

To get a feel for how much money you are going to need to live in retirement, you need to understand just how much your retirement will cost and how much savings you will need. Read through the following worksheet and gather the data required to complete the exercise. When you have it all in front of you, get out your calculator.

**Retirement Funds Needed at 65 to Keep Equivalent of Current Income**

| Age | Current Salary | At Age 65 | Social Security | SS and Pension |
|-----|---------------|-----------|----------------|----------------|
| 40 | $40,000 | $102,532 | $164,463 | $14,592 |
|    | $60,000 | $153,798 | $482,903 | $274,825 |
|    | $80,000 | $205,064 | $965,110 | $692,237 |
|    | $100,000 | $256,330 | $1,441,310 | $1,105,701 |
| 50 | $40,000 | $69,267 | $111,163 | $11,470 |
|    | $60,000 | $103,901 | $337,529 | $199,644 |
|    | $80,000 | $138,534 | $655,614 | $475,144 |
|    | $100,000 | $173,168 | $968,966 | $747,337 |
| 60 | $40,000 | $46,794 | $74,902 | $8,778 |
|    | $60,000 | $70,192 | $243,189 | $152,137 |
|    | $80,000 | $93,589 | $451,975 | $333,021 |
|    | $100,000 | $116,986 | $657,108 | $511,338 |

This table assumes a 20-year retirement, 4 percent inflation, retirement income equal to 70 percent of preretirement earnings, maximum Social Security benefit for worker and spouse, a pension equal to 35 percent of preretirement income, and an 8 percent pretax return during retirement.

*Source: SunAmerica Financial Inc. 1996*

# ARE YOU SAVING ENOUGH FOR RETIREMENT?

Now you need to find out how much money you'll have to put away to reach these numbers. The following worksheet can help you estimate how much you might need to save for retirement in today's dollars. (For a more complete analysis, you may want to contact a financial planner. See Chapter 19.)

## *Getting Started*

A. Estimate your yearly pension after you retire. Your company's pension statement may give you an amount; if not, estimate what that figure will be and enter that number here. $_____

B. Estimate your yearly Social Security benefits by using the following chart, and enter that number here. (To get a more exact figure, call the Social Security Administration at 800-772-1213.) $_____

C. Add lines A and B and enter here. This is the total income you will receive from your pension and Social Security. $_____

## *The Size of Your Nest Egg*

1. How much will you need to live on each year after retirement? (Experts suggest multiplying your current income by .8 or 80 percent.) $_____

2. Enter the amount you will get each year from Social Security and your pension here (line C). $_____

3. How much will you need to earn from investments each year after you retire? (Subtract line 2 from line 1.) $_____

4. How many years will you be in retirement? (Many experts say you should plan to live into your 90s.)

_____

5. What average yearly rate of real return (for simplicity, use 4%) do you expect from your savings/investments after you retire? $_____

6. Look at the following table and find the percentage you wrote on line 5. Then read across in that row to find the figure listed under the number of years you expect to be in retirement (from line 4). Enter that number here. $_____

**Number of Years in Retirement**

|     | 1 | 5 | 10 | 15 | 20 | 25 | 30 |
|-----|-----|------|------|-------|-------|-------|-------|
| 1% | .99 | 4.85 | 9.47 | 13.87 | 18.05 | 22.02 | 25.81 |
| 2% | .98 | 4.71 | 8.98 | 12.85 | 16.35 | 19.52 | 22.40 |
| 3% | .97 | 4.58 | 8.53 | 11.94 | 14.88 | 17.41 | 19.60 |
| 4% | .96 | 4.45 | 8.11 | 11.12 | 13.59 | 15.62 | 17.29 |
| 5% | .95 | 4.33 | 7.72 | 10.38 | 12.46 | 14.09 | 15.37 |

7. Multiply line 6 by line 3. This is an estimate of how much money you will need to have at retirement in today's dollars. Your earnings from this nest egg, along with your pension and Social Security benefits, will provide your retirement income. $_____

*Determine a Savings Goal*

8. How many years are left before you retire? _____

9. What annual real return (your return minus inflation) do you expect from your savings/investments between now and when you retire? _____

10. Look in the left-hand column of the table below and find the percentage you wrote in line 9. Read across in that row to find the figure listed under the number of years left until you retire. Write that number here. _____

**NUMBER OF YEARS UNTIL RETIREMENT**

|     | 1     | 5     | 10    | 15    | 20    | 25    | 30    |
|-----|-------|-------|-------|-------|-------|-------|-------|
| 2%  | 1.020 | 1.104 | 1.219 | 1.346 | 1.486 | 1.641 | 1.811 |
| 3%  | 1.030 | 1.159 | 1.344 | 1.558 | 1.806 | 2.094 | 2.427 |
| 4%  | 1.040 | 1.217 | 1.480 | 1.801 | 2.191 | 2.666 | 3.243 |
| 5%  | 1.050 | 1.276 | 1.629 | 2.079 | 2.653 | 3.386 | 4.322 |
| 6%  | 1.060 | 1.338 | 1.791 | 2.397 | 3.207 | 4.292 | 5.743 |

11. Add up all your savings (don't count the pension benefits listed previously under Getting Started). Include the money in your savings accounts, your 401(k) plan, your IRA, and other investments here. $_____

12. Multiply your total assets (line 11) by the number on line 10. This is what the savings/investments you have now will be worth when you retire. $_____

13. Subtract line 12 from line 7 and write the result here. This is how much more you need to save for retirement. $_____

*How It All Comes Together*

14. What is your yearly salary? $_____

15. Enter the number you wrote on line 13. $_____

16. Enter the percentage you wrote on line 9 here. _____ Find that percentage in the left-hand column in the table below. Read across the row until you reach the number listed in the column under the number of years that are left until you retire. Enter that number here. _____

**NUMBER OF YEARS UNTIL RETIREMENT**

| | 1 | 5 | 10 | 15 | 20 | 25 | 30 |
|------|------|------|-------|-------|-------|-------|-------|
| 2% | 1.02 | 5.31 | 11.17 | 17.64 | 24.78 | 32.67 | 41.38 |
| 3% | 1.03 | 5.47 | 11.81 | 19.16 | 27.68 | 37.55 | 49.00 |
| 4% | 1.04 | 5.63 | 12.49 | 20.82 | 30.97 | 43.31 | 58.33 |
| 5% | 1.05 | 5.80 | 13.21 | 22.66 | 34.72 | 50.11 | 69.76 |
| 6% | 1.06 | 5.98 | 13.97 | 24.67 | 38.99 | 58.16 | 83.80 |

17. Multiply line 14 (yearly salary) by line 16 and put that number here. $_____

18. Divide line 13 by line 17 and put the result here. _____ Multiply by 100 and put that number here. This is the percentage of your annual salary that you need to save to meet your retirement goal. The amount will need to increase each year to keep up with inflation. _____%

*Source: Fidelity Investments*

In this lesson, you learned how to estimate how much money
you will need annually to maintain your current lifestyle in
retirement. You also learned how much you'll have to save to
reach your goal. In the next lesson, you will begin to learn
about the types of long-term investments you can choose from
to build your nest egg.

# LEARNING THE BASICS OF SAVING AND INVESTING

*In this lesson, you'll become more knowledgeable about the different types of investments suitable for your retirement savings.*

## SAFE INVESTMENTS VERSUS RISKY ONES

To start investing, you'll need to understand why a riskier investment is usually better over the long term—which is more than five years—than a safe investment. Playing it safe can cost you in the long run. It's also very important that you start saving early to take advantage of compounding.

**Compounding** Compounding is when interest is added to interest already earned on your principle investment.

All those years of compounding can make even a small $2,000 investment into a substantial sum over a 30-year time frame.

The following table shows you how an investment of just $2,000 at age 30, earning 4 percent annually, can grow.

| AGE | INVESTMENT |
|-----|------------|
| 30  | $2,000     |
| 40  | $24,012    |
| 50  | $59,556    |
| 60  | $112,170   |

*Source: The U.S. Department of Labor*

To invest wisely, you'll need to have a working understanding of several investment terms. There are three things to consider before making any investment:

- *Liquidity.* How fast can you get your hands on the money and its earnings?

- *Safety.* Will you get all your money back?

- *Rate of return.* How much will your money earn?

Simply put, the safer your money, the less it will earn. The riskier the investment, the higher the potential earnings. The goal is to balance your investments between the two extremes. The younger you are, the more risk you can tolerate. But even when you are nearing retirement, you can't afford to play it completely safe with low-risk/low-return investments or inflation will devour your hard-earned savings.

The right mix of investments for your plan depends on how many years remain until your retirement and how old you are now. Your investment risk will also be determined by your personal tolerance for risk.

The following table shows how you might want to allocate your investments in relation to your age.

**Investment Allocations According to Your Age**

| Age | 20s | 30s | 40s | 50s | 60s |
|---|---|---|---|---|---|
| Stocks or stock mutual funds | 80% | 70% | 60% | 50% | 30% to 40% |
| Bonds or bond mutual funds | 20% long- or inter-mediate-term bonds | 30% fixed-income bonds | 40% | 50% | 40% to 50% |
| CDs and money market accounts or funds | none | none | none | none | 20% to 30% |

# How Bonds Work

When you buy a bond, you are in essence making a loan to the issuer, whether it's the federal government or a corporation. In return, the government or corporation, depending on the type of bond, agrees to pay interest at specific intervals, typically, twice a year, until the bond matures. Then the principal amount, or face value, is repaid in full. Bonds are rated for safety by rating agencies such as Moody's Investors Services and Standard and Poor's. The ratings range from AAA for the safest to D for the riskiest. Investing in bonds is for the long-term because prices will fluctuate as interest rates change. As interest rates rise, the value of the bonds fall and vice versa. The money that you put in bonds should always be held to maturity.

**Bond**  A bond is a type of investment that typically has a fixed rate of return and pays out a set amount of income annually over a set time period.

There are several types of bonds available to investors. You can buy bonds through a broker. U.S. Treasury notes or bonds, however, can be purchased directly from the government through a program called Treasury Direct without a service fee.

*tip*  You can learn more about Treasury Direct by calling the Federal Reserve bank nearest you. To find a bank, you can either write The Bureau of Public Debt, Department F, Department of the Treasury, Washington, D.C. 20239-11200, or call 202-874-4000.

Here are the major categories of bonds:

- *U.S. Treasuries.* Treasury bills come in maturities of 60 days to one year. Treasury notes run one year to 10 years, and Treasury bonds mature in two to 20 year time spans. They are considered the safest bonds because they are backed by the federal government.

Notes of less than four years start with a $5,000 minimum. Longer term notes and bonds start with a $1,000 minimum. Interest is paid semiannually and is free from state and local taxes. The shorter the maturity period, the lower the interest rate. These bonds are best for people nearing retirement or very conservative investors.

- *Municipal bonds.* These bonds are issued by state and local governments, and the interest is free from federal taxes. Since these bonds are already tax-exempt, these are not good investments for an IRA or Keogh plan.

- *Corporate bonds.* These bonds are issued by corporations and are riskier than Treasuries, but in return pay higher rates. Corporate bonds with very low ratings, or sometimes no rating, are known as junk bonds.

  Because they are so risky, these are not always suitable for retirement savings. The bonds are usually sold in increments of $1,000 with interest paid out twice a year.

- *Zero coupon bonds.* Zeros pay interest only at maturity and come in face values starting at $1,000, but are actually sold at steep discounts of as much as 80 percent of that face value, depending on the maturity date. Although you don't actually get the interest each year, the government does levy annual taxes on that accrued interest. For that reason, zeros often work best in a Keogh or IRA that is tax-sheltered.

# How CDs Work

The longer the time period you invest for, the higher the interest you will receive. If you withdraw your money from a CD before the allotted time, you are usually hit with a penalty. Interest rates vary from bank to bank, but are typically low. On a national average, rates might be from 4 percent for a 3-month CD, 4.9 percent for a 1-year CD, and as high as 5.42 percent for a 5-year CD.

**Certificate of Deposit (CD)**   A CD is a bank deposit with a guaranteed rate of interest for a set period, typically 3-month, 6-month, 1-year, or 5-year.

What makes these investments so safe is that, providing the CD is deposited in a federally insured institution, the government guarantees up to $100,000. Moreover, because it is easy to invest directly in a CD without going through a broker, you pay no extra commissions. The upside of a CD is that it's relatively liquid. The downside is that because it earns low interest rates, it isn't the best place to park your retirement money for the long haul.

# How Money Market Accounts Work

Money markets pay out a relatively meager percentage, recently around 2.85 percent. Similar to a CD, if the account is with a federally insured institution, the funds are insured up to $100,000. It's better than stashing your savings under the mattress, but not by much when you figure in the cost of taxes and inflation erosion. Your best bet is to use these solely as cash emergency funds.

 **Money Market Account**   A money market account is a bank savings account that pays slightly higher interest than a basic savings account and has no set time period.

In this lesson, you learned the value of starting to invest early and the difference between safe and risky investments and how they fit into a retirement plan. In the next lesson, you'll learn about riskier investments, such as stocks, that provide greater returns.

# THE BASICS OF INVESTING IN STOCKS

*In this lesson, you'll learn what stock shares are and why they are an important part of your retirement nest egg.*

## WHAT ARE STOCKS?

Investing in common stocks means more risk, or volatility, over the short haul. However, in the long run, they have usually provided the biggest returns and the highest margin over inflation. A portfolio that includes stocks or stock mutual funds has the potential to earn a far greater return than one that is invested solely in fixed-interest rate investments. You should make shares of stock in a publicly held company the centerpiece of your retirement savings. Stocks will always do better than bonds over any long-term investing period.

*Stocks* are shares in a company that are sold to raise money for the company. There are more than 8,000 companies whose shares trade on one of the three big stock exchanges. The three exchanges are:

- The New York Stock Exchange, which trades most of the country's largest corporations, has around 2,579 listed firms.

- The American Stock Exchange has 755 listed companies, and the firms tend to be somewhat smaller than the NYSE member firms.

- The National Association of Securities Dealers Automated Quotation system, or NASDAQ, has some 5,036 member companies. NASDAQ companies are generally smaller than the other two exchanges' members and are often start-ups or new ventures.

On any given day, some 600 million shares of stock are bought and sold on the three exchanges. Picking individual stocks is an art form that can take years to perfect and often requires a strong stomach. Prices of stocks can fluctuate for many reasons that may have nothing at all to do with the company's performance or products. Overall bad economic news out of Washington can send shares plummeting southward or, at times, zipping north. A rumor of a potential takeover by a competitor can send shares skyrocketing. Even professional stockpickers get burned now and again. But no one can afford to ignore investing in stocks.

While it's true that stocks can swing widely over the short-term, they have still outperformed interest-paying investments over every 20-year period since 1931. The minimum percentage of your investments in stocks should equal 100 minus your age: thus a 40-year-old should have at least 60 percent of her portfolio in stocks. As retirement nears, you can shift more money into some of the fixed-interest investments discussed in Lesson 3, but don't abandon stocks. You'll need the growth to protect yourself from the impact of inflation.

### COMPARING INVESTMENTS

| ASSET | AVERAGE ANNUAL RETURN |
| --- | --- |
| Small-company stocks | 12.36% |
| Common stocks | 10.38% |
| Long-term government bonds | 5.02% |
| U.S. Treasury bills | 3.69% |
| Inflation | 3.13% |

*Source: 1926–1993 returns*

Many common stocks pay dividends. But patient investors know that it is better to avoid taking dividends in cash to help pay current expenses. Reinvesting those dividends to purchase more shares of the stock will help your investment continue to grow.

**Dividends**   Dividends are the company's profits that it distributes to investors. You'll often hear investment advisors discuss a particular stock's yield. Yield is calculated by dividing the current annual dividend rate by the share price. For example, a stock that is selling at $40 that pays annual dividends of $1.00 a share has a yield of 2.5 percent. The dividend and yield are usually listed in the newspaper stock listings.

# How to Buy Stocks

Typically, stocks are bought and sold through a stockbroker, who charges a commission of 2 percent or so for his or her services. You will usually pay a lower fee if you purchase in lots of 100 shares at a time. Moreover, discount brokers such as Charles Schwab and Quick & Reilly, will lower those fees by 70 percent, providing you aren't looking for any type of investment advice in making your selection.

However, there are now 120-plus no-load stocks, or direct purchase plans, that sell shares directly to you. Roughly half of these companies are utilities, and some limit the option to their own customers. You can usually buy the stocks for an initial investment of anywhere from $20 to $1,500. To buy a stock this way you need to call the company and ask them to send you a registration form. Then you fill it in and send it along with your check. More and more companies are letting investors buy shares directly from them with no broker's fee. These include Barnett Banks, Exxon Corp., Florida Progress, McDonald's, Wal-Mart, and Home Depot.

 **tip**    To get a list of companies that permit you to buy directly, you can write to the National Association of Investors Corp., 1515 E. Eleven Mile Road, Royal Oak, Michigan 48067.

There are dozens of ways to choose what stocks to buy (which you'll explore in later lessons), but the key to making any investment is to educate yourself before you invest your hard-earned savings. Don't put all your eggs in one basket. You'll want to spread out your stock investments among a variety of industries and risk-levels. Diversification is the key to long-term investing. Before you get started, though, ask yourself several questions:

- How much will it cost?

- Will this stock fit into my overall retirement plan?

- What is the company's track record over the last five years or so? You can find this information in the annual report or 10(k).

- Does it make sense on a gut level?

- Is the potential worth the risk?

Here are four categories of stocks:

- *Blue-chip stocks.* These are the crème de la crème of the stock world with solid, first-rate financial underpinnings. They are usually large, well-established companies that pay dividends, which are raised annually, and are among the most reliable stocks to own. Some blue-chip stocks include AT&T, General Motors, and Xerox. These companies are usually listed on the New York Stock Exchange or the American Stock Exchange.

- *Income stocks.* These equities are among the best moneymakers for your retirement account. The companies typically pay out anywhere from 50 percent to 75 percent of profits in the form of quarterly dividends to investors. The prices of these stocks don't appreciate much, but the dividends produce constant returns.

- *Small-company stocks.* These are often called growth stocks because they are smaller companies with the potential to grow faster than the overall economy. They are often young, fast-growing firms that trade on the NASDAQ over-the-counter market. They are riskier than a blue-chip or income stock. Even so, if you can weather volatile prices over the short run, you'll stand a good chance of being rewarded by substantial price appreciation over the long haul. In the last 35 years, small company stocks gained nearly 14 percent annually, as compared to 10.4 percent for the 500 largest U.S. stocks.

- *Foreign stocks.* Investing in shares of foreign companies is a good way to diversify your retirement investments, or portfolio. U.S. companies make up just half of all the stocks available worldwide. Because of the currency risk (the valuation of, say French francs against the dollar, can fluctuate daily), however, these stocks can be riskier than American ones. It is easy today to buy foreign shares on the major U.S. exchanges without having to trade on a foreign exchange. In fact, hundreds of foreign companies sell their shares here in the form of ADRs, or American Depository Receipts. Small investors, though, are probably better off investing in international equities through an international mutual fund.

# WHERE TO LEARN MORE ABOUT A PARTICULAR STOCK

In the United States, companies must provide a vast amount of information about their finances to investors. To help you do your homework, you can start by calling the company itself and asking to be connected to the shareholders relations department. At your request, they will send you the company's most recent annual report, which will contain its balance sheets and most recent profit and loss statement. Next stop: the nearest library. Most public libraries have the Value Line Investment Survey and Standard & Poor's stock reports. Each of these volumes offers in-depth data and analyst evaluations on literally thousands of publicly traded companies. Value Line lists roughly 1,700 stocks, and S&P lists more than 4,600. You'll learn about the company's future, as well as its financial history going back a decade or more. Even so, buying individual stocks is traumatic for many people. The value of your investment relies on thousands of things you can't control.

In this lesson, you learned the basics of investing in stocks to build your retirement nest egg. In the next lesson, you'll learn the critical role mutual funds play in your retirement plan.

# 6

# THE WONDER OF MUTUAL FUNDS

*In this lesson, you will learn the important role that mutual funds play in piecing together a successful retirement plan.*

## THE BASICS OF MUTUAL FUNDS

While you understand what a major part equities must play in your retirement savings, you may not have the stomach to ride out the highs and lows of the stock market. Fortunately, there's another way to meet that goal—and have a bit more peace of mind.

## WHAT'S A MUTUAL FUND?

A *mutual fund* is a group of stocks, bonds, or a mixture of investments that are pooled together and managed by a professional money manager of an investment company. The pool is divided into shares and sold to investors. A typical minimum investment is $1,500, but you can find funds that require an initial investment of just $250. Moreover, the initial investment could be even lower if you sign up for a monthly deduction from your checking or savings account. These automatic monthly investment programs may only require $50 a month to get started.

Like a stock, the share prices of a mutual fund, called the *net asset value*, shift up and down daily. As with stocks you do take a risk that the value of your fund will fall. But, using mutual funds allows you to spread your $1,500—and the risk—among a number of stocks. The advantages of diversification and the low minimum investment let you invest small amounts regularly, which is a perfect way to accumulate money for the long term.

Today, there are around 7,000 funds with a range of investment goals and strategies from which to choose. A fund might own a selection of foreign stocks, blue-chip, or small company stocks.

## CHOOSING THE RIGHT FUNDS

There are several major mutual fund investment categories that you might want to include in your retirement plan:

- *Aggressive growth/small company.* These funds invest in small companies that are frequently operating in cutting-edge industries such as the high-tech industry. They do not produce significant income or dividends. On one hand, they carry significant risk because they are so young. On the other hand, they have the potential of achieving tremendous price appreciation as they expand and grow. This is a long-term investment that you should hold for seven or more years.

- *Balanced.* Just as the name indicates, these funds balance their portfolios between stocks and bonds.

They usually pay dividends and aim to conserve your initial principal. This is a mid-to-long-term investment that you should hang on to for five to ten years.

- *Growth.* Long-term appreciation is the goal with these funds. They invest in well-established companies boasting stock prices that are likely to beat inflation. They normally don't pay dividends. This is considered a long-term investment that you will want to hold for seven or more years.

- *Income.* These funds invest in the shares of firms that typically pay dividends, such as utilities or phone companies.

- *Growth and income.* These funds invest in a combination of well-established companies and dividend-payers. The goal of these funds is to balance the objectives of long-term growth and current income. This is an investment that you should look at as worth holding for a minimum of seven years.

- *Index funds.* Fund managers build their fund portfolio by matching an existing index like the Standard & Poor's 500 stock index, which invests in 500 big-company stocks. The Index funds are a good mid-to-long-term investment of five to ten years.

- *International and global stock.* These funds invest in stocks of non-U.S. companies. Some funds specialize in companies from a single country such as Mexico or Japan, or a region such as Latin America, Europe, or Asia.

- *Socially-conscious.* These funds invest in firms that have an excellent environmental record or don't make or sell politically incorrect goods such as guns, alcohol, tobacco, and so forth.

- *Sector.* The objective of these funds is to invest solely in a single industry, say technology or automobiles. These funds are another long-term holding of seven or more years.

- *Bond funds.* There are several different categories of bond funds. High-grade corporate bond funds invest in bonds issued by top-rated companies. U.S. government bond funds invest in U.S. Treasuries with either short-term, intermediate, or long-term maturities. There are international bond funds as well. Mortgage-backed funds invest in securities issued by the Government National Mortgage Association (GNMAs). In general, these are considered to be mid-to-long-term investments.

- *Money market funds.* These funds are designed to keep your principal intact by investing in conservative investments such as CDs and Treasuries. These should be considered a short-term investment of no more than three years.

The following table shows you how these various mutual funds have performed historically and their cumulative total return in dollars each year.

## PERFORMANCE OF MUTUAL FUNDS

| TYPE OF FUND | 12/31/69-12/31/70 | 12/31/79-12/31/80 | 12/31/89-12/31/90 | 12/31/94-12/31/95 |
|---|---|---|---|---|
| Corporate Bond A rated | 4.93 | 2.16 | 6.79 | 18.66 |
| Balanced Funds | 5.77 | 19.51 | –0.12 | 25.39 |
| Corporate Bond BBB rated | 9.70 | –0.68 | 4.89 | 20.18 |
| Growth Funds | –7.87 | 36.76 | –4.51 | 30.70 |
| General Bond Funds | 8.81 | 8.30 | 1.76 | 17.67 |
| Growth & Income Funds | –0.83 | 27.76 | –4.23 | 31.03 |
| Global Funds | –6.90 | 32.16 | –9.67 | 16.10 |
| GNMA Funds | n/a | –4.69 | 9.55 | 16.37 |
| Income Funds | 4.69 | 17.64 | –0.60 | 22.63 |
| Small Company Growth Funds | –19.23 | 46.43 | –10.32 | 31.86 |
| Utility Funds | 13.46 | 6.42 | –1.06 | 27.36 |

*Source: Lipper Analytical Services*

# WHERE TO BUY MUTUAL FUNDS

You can buy mutual funds either from a broker or directly from the fund. Most funds have 800 telephone numbers that you can call and request a prospectus that gives you a summary of the fund's objectives and past performance. They also tell you what management fees they may charge to handle your money.

*Load mutual funds* charge you an initial fee to buy the shares. These fees can range from 1 percent to as high as 8 percent. In addition to the upfront load, you should watch out for the backend load that some funds may charge if you sell your holdings within five to seven years. Funds that are sold without upfront fees or commissions are called *no-load mutual funds*.

*12b-1 fees* are a main element of funds with high expenses. These are charges that a fund levies to cover their marketing and sales expenses. These fees range from .25 percent to 1 percent of assets annually. You'll want to avoid funds that charge more than .25 percent for this.

Buying shares is easy. You request a prospectus from the fund company by telephone and wait for it to arrive in the mail. Then read the materials carefully, fill out the application, and mail in your check. Most funds let you automatically reinvest your earnings by buying more shares. This is a great way to boost your savings because it keeps you investing without even thinking about it.

In this lesson, you learned what a mutual fund is and what the major types of funds are. In the next lesson, you will learn how variable annuities can fit into your nest egg.

# 7

# Taking Advantage of Tax-Deferred Annuities

*In this lesson, you'll learn how to tap into the tax benefits of investing in annuities.*

## What Is an Annuity?

The best way to understand an annuity is to think of it as the opposite of a life insurance policy. Its primary purpose is to provide income to people who think they might outlive their retirement financial resources. It is supplementary retirement income above what you will get from your Individual Retirement Account, Social Security, pension, and other investments. With life insurance, you shell out regular payments so that when you die, your survivors get the proceeds. With an annuity, you pay in periodic payments, or one lump sum, toward a time when you receive monthly distributions for the rest of your life. Those funds can start coming your way at retirement. However, you might opt to delay those distributions. Some contracts allow you to push it back until age 85.

**Annuities**　Annuities are a tax-deferred invest-ment with an insurance company that lets you earn interest and also provides a death benefit.

Here's how it works:

In general, when you buy an annuity you write a lump sum check for a minimum of $1,000 to, say, a maximum of $10,000 to a financial planner, broker, or insurance agent. The insurance company then issues you an annuity contract and agrees to pay you a certain amount of cash at a specified date in the future. That sum depends on your age and the prevailing interest rates. Like an IRA account, an annuity earns money that compounds substantially over time and is tax-deferred. There's no limit to the amount you can invest annually, and you aren't required to start withdrawing the funds at any set age. Some companies offer flexible-premium annuities that allow you to continually put more money into your annuity in payments as low as $25 a month.

There are some drawbacks, though. The biggest problem with an annuity is the various fees that insurers charge you. For instance, the insurance company that issues the annuity may hit you with a fine—known as a surrender fee—for as much as 7 percent for early withdrawals if it is less than five years after you buy the annuity. Sometimes the surrender charge period lasts as long as 12 years. As a result, you should plan to hang on to the annuity for at least a decade. But even if they let you pull out of the original investment free of penalty, the IRS will demand 10 percent, providing you are younger than age 59 1/2. Then too, annuities can be expensive right from the get go. Some insurers charge as high as 4 percent in sales com-missions. That fee is taken out before your money even begins to earn interest. Find out before you buy if there are front-end sales charges, or loads. Several companies have started to drop these, but some still have them. You will also need to ask if they charge annual administrative fees at a flat rate, say, $25.

Annuities are not federally insured. It's important to do business with a healthy, solvent insurer. Thus, it's important to understand the financial underpinnings of any insurance company before you invest. Understanding complex balance sheets is not required, but you must carefully run a check on the insurance company's safety rating. A+ or AAA are the highest ratings. A.M. Best (908-439-2200), Moody's Investors Service (212-553-0377), Standard & Poor's (212-208-1527), and Weiss Research (800-289-9222) all rate insurance companies for safety and solvency. Weiss, in particular, takes a critical look at an insurance company's finances. And with Weiss, you can get a report via telephone for $15 per company. Many experts say an A or better rating is sufficient, but to be on the safe side, look for a minimum of A+. If your salesperson can't show you these evaluations, you can find them in the public library, or call the rating service directly.

There's another factor to consider when you're comparing annuities. As stated earlier, some funds charge high annual expense fees. Look for low total management expenses—those that charge below 2 percent each year are considered low.

*tip*    For a list of low-load insurers in your city, call the Fee for Service annuity brokerage at 800-874-5662.

## EVALUATING THE TYPES OF ANNUITIES

There are two kinds of annuities: immediate annuities and deferred annuities. With an immediate annuity, you invest a lump sum, and it begins to pay out monthly right away. Typically, what happens is that someone who gets a lump-sum distribution from an IRA or pension plan rolls it over into an immediate annuity. A lot of retired people choose to do this for tax purposes because the money is taxed only as you withdraw it.

With deferred annuities, you can choose to withdraw your money in one payout or a series of payouts at some future date. Moreover, with a deferred annuity, you decide whether you want to have a fixed interest rate, one that is set for a time period of up to ten years, or a variable rate that invests in riskier, but potentially more lucrative vehicles, such as equity or bond mutual funds. The downside of variables is that there is no way to calculate what you will actually receive at payout.

## WITHDRAWING THE FUNDS

If you want to jump from one annuity to another, without paying taxes, you can switch your annuity to a new insurer by using 1035(a) of the IRS Tax Code. It lets you make a direct transfer from one insurance company to another. You fill out the forms with the new firm and write to your current insurance company requesting that they transfer the account to the new firm. You save on taxes, but beware, your insurer might still dock you for an early withdrawal.

If you want to withdraw the money from a deferred annuity before age 59 1/2, you'll usually be hit with a 10 percent federal tax penalty on the interest earned on your principal investment. You won't, however, be fined on the principal. Then again, you may be hit by those surrender fees we discussed earlier. In general, that charge ranges from 5 to 15 percent of your total investment the first year and drops 1 percent per year thereafter. Some firms will let you take out 10 percent of your account's value each year without penalty.

Whether you have opted for a fixed or variable rate, there are many payout options when taking money from an annuity. Here are some of the most popular ways:

- *Life annuity.* Your insurance company will send you a fixed sum monthly or annually as long as you live. However, if you die before the money has all been paid out, the insurer keeps the balance.

- *Systematic withdrawal.* This option lets you tell the insurance company exactly when you want to get your check: monthly, quarterly, or annually. You can instruct them to send you just the monthly interest or a certain dollar figure. Moreover, you can make changes in the amount or payment schedule whenever you want.

- *Joint-and-survivor.* This provision makes sure that your spouse or any other dependent keeps getting paid after you die.

In this lesson, you learned how annuities act as tax-deferred compounding investments to help your retirement money grow dramatically over time. In the next lesson, you'll learn about another popular retirement investment, a Guaranteed-Income Contract, or GIC.

# Investing in Guaranteed Investment Contracts and Employee Stock Ownership Plans

*In this lesson, you'll learn the pros and cons of investing your retirement money in Guaranteed Investment Contracts (GICs) and Employee Stock Ownership Plans (ESOPs).*

## Investing in Guaranteed Investment Contracts (GICs)

Nearly 75 percent of all 401(k) plans offer GICs as an investment choice for employees, and most plan participants select them. In fact, $6 out of every $10 that is invested in 401(k) plans today goes into GICs.

**Guaranteed Investment Contract (GIC)**   A GIC is a fixed-interest investment issued by an insurance company that lasts between one and seven years.

Don't be confused by the word "guaranteed." GICs are not insured by the federal government and are only as solid as the insurance company that issues them. What is *guaranteed* is the interest rate for the first year.

To avoid the risk of an insurer going belly-up and plan participants losing their retirement funds, some 401(k) managers buy two dozen or so separate GICs and combine them into one GIC fund. That way the risk is spread across many insurers.

## How Do GICs Work?

To spread risk, your plan manager may buy contracts from more than a dozen insurers. This way they can mix several rates of return at various maturities. The insurers will then invest GIC assets in bonds, both government and corporate, even high-yielding junk bonds. They charge a fee, which is usually taken as a piece of the income from these various investments. The yield you get is usually on par with CDs and a bit higher, say, one percentage point more, than you'd get from a Treasury note yield. When your GIC expires or matures, your plan manager reinvests it in another GIC. Retirees, or someone cashing out of the plan, would get their principal and interest back.

## Why Are GICs So Popular?

GICs remain one the most popular investments within a 401(k) retirement plan. Today, more than half of all employee-directed 401(k) assets are invested in GICs. That's because most people make the mistake of thinking that GICs are as safe as a CD, which is backed by the federal government. Not only are they not guaranteed to be safe, but GICs are among the lowest paying selections you can make, usually earning interest of no more than 5 percent annually. While that may be better than Treasuries for the fixed-income part of your portfolio, for most of you, it's still a far too conservative investment.

If you are still interested in investing your retirement income in a GIC, there's some homework you should do first before making this selection:

- First, ask your plan manager to provide you with the names of the insurers they buy contracts from.

- Then track down the insurance company's credit rating. Most pension plans buy only from insurers with ratings of A or better.

- Be sure that your plan manager is buying GICs from several insurers, which lowers the risk of one of the insurers failing.

Remember that if one insurer failed, your assets probably wouldn't take much of a hit. That's providing the GICs are written with at least a half-dozen companies. Moreover, in most states GIC holders would be able to recover some money from the state because investments would be covered under the same terms as holders of life insurance.

## THE REAL PROBLEM WITH GICs

In reality, it's not the threat that an insurer will bite the dust that is so troubling about GICs from a retirement perspective. The real drawback is that the yields are so low and for young people to lock their retirement funds in such a plodder is not advisable. Only as you get closer to retirement, say 50 or so, would you want to consider GICs as an option.

## WHAT'S A BIC?

Some employers are now offering Bank Investment Contracts, or BICs, as an alternative to GICs. Because these are bank deposits, the funds are federally insured up to $100,000.

# INVESTING IN EMPLOYEE STOCK OWNERSHIP PLANS (ESOPS)

For employees, Employee Stock Ownership Plans, or ESOPs, are an easy way to buy stock without paying any commissions to a brokerage house. However, when you leave the firm, you take possession of the shares and face paying taxes on the current value. Up until that time, the stock can appreciate tax-free.

**Employee Stock Ownership Plan (ESOP)**
As the name suggests, an ESOP is a pension plan that allows employees to buy stock in the company itself. This might be done through payroll withholding from your salary, or your employers might give you a given number of shares each year as part of your annual salary.

The best thing to do if you own company stock and are leaving is to roll the funds into an IRA.

## HOW DOES AN ESOP WORK?

Your employer kicks in a certain percentage of your pay as an ESOP-participating employee, usually between 8 and 15 percent of your annual salary, or you ask for a percentage of your salary to be deducted pre-tax and automatically invested in shares.

## WHAT ARE THE DRAWBACKS OF AN ESOP?

ESOPs often sound better than they are for retirement plan purposes. An ESOP is not a diversified investment, so you are rolling the dice. That's because while the prices of some company stocks take off and may be a good investment, others remain flat or drop. Market fluctuations mean there is no guarantee what the return will be when you are ready to cash out. Today, blue-chip firms such as Polaroid and Procter & Gamble offer these plans to their employees, but there are plenty of smaller, riskier firms offering them as well. Since you are already depending on your employer for your annual compensation, it doesn't make sense to have all your eggs in one basket.

## CAN YOU DIVERSIFY AN ESOP?

You can diversify your ESOP account as you get closer to retiring. At age 55, if you have been in the ESOP for at least ten years, you can request that 25 percent of your assets be shifted to investments outside the company stock. It is usually paid to you directly in cash so you can roll it over into another tax-deferred account such as an IRA. At age 60, you are permitted to move 50 percent of your holdings outside company stock.

In this lesson, you learned about investing your retirement money into GICs and ESOPs. In the next lesson, you will learn some easy ways to begin choosing some riskier investments.

# BECOMING A RISK TAKER

*In this lesson, you'll learn about ways to become a braver investor.*

## GETTING STARTED AS A RISK TAKER

In general, women are so worried about making a bad investment choice that they freeze. When men make an investment mistake, they'll typically put the blame on their broker, financial planner, or shrug it off to a bit of bad luck. On the other hand, women tend to take it personally and blame themselves.

Therefore, it's no surprise that many women pick conservative investments like money market accounts and CDs, which don't lose money. They shy away from investing in individual stocks or stock mutual funds.

That's a devastating mistake if you are investing for the long-term for your retirement.

## START SMALL

The best way to gird your financial nerves is to start small. Try setting aside, say, five percent, of your paycheck for your first investment. That way, if the worst thing happens and you have a setback, you won't be wiped out.

## SAVING ON COMMISSIONS

About 150 blue-chip companies, such as Exxon and Johnson Controls, let first-time investors buy shares directly from them, for as little as $50 to $100, at no commission. After you are in the program, you can usually invest as little as $10 to $20 at a time to accumulate additional shares. There are also hundreds of stock mutual funds that require low minimum investments.

 A list of these programs is available free of charge by writing Dow Theory Forecasts Inc., 7412 Calumet Avenue, Hammond, Indiana 46324-2692.

A stock dividend-reinvestment plan, called a DRIP, is another terrific way to add to your shareholdings without going through a broker. Roughly 900 publicly traded companies offer DRIPs, which reinvest your dividends back into shares. Some even discount their share prices by up to 5 percent for current shareholders. For a listing of firms that offer DRIPs, you might want to order the Directory of Companies Offering Dividend Reinvestment Plans (Evergreen Enterprises, P.O. Box 763, Laurel, MD 20725; $32.45).

By eliminating commissions, you are saving more than you would imagine. The commission charged by full-service stockbrokers, such as Dean Witter, Merrill Lynch, or Prudential Securities, is usually about 2 percent of the stock price. For an over-the-counter stock that trades lightly you may be charged nearly 5 percent. If you buy 100 shares at a time, called a round lot, you'll pay less in commission than if you buy fewer shares, called odd-lots. Moreover, the more expensive the stock is, the lower your commission is likely to be. Big brokerages usually have a minimum commission charge of, say, $35 per order.

One reason investors go to a full-service firm is for advice on what to buy and when. Your broker will provide you with a company's financial statements and prospectuses, as well as analyst reports on the firms. But always remember, brokers are salespeople who make the lion's share of their income by commissions. Listen to their recommendations, but always do your own research and homework.

It's possible to shave commissions by buying and selling shares through a national discount brokerage firm, such as Charles Schwab & Co. (800-648-5300), Fidelity Investments (800-544-7272), Jack White & Co. (800-522-5944), and Quick and Reilly (800-222-0437). These discounters will have minimum commissions per transaction just like the full-service houses do. They may even be slightly higher, say, $39 per order at Charles Schwab. But providing you are buying a large enough quantity of stock, these discounters will cut commissions per share 50 to 70 percent lower than a full-service brokerage. However, they offer no advice on what to select.

Take a look at the following table to see how the commissions that you may pay compare.

| 100 shares/$100 each | Full-service | $106 |
|---|---|---|
| 100 shares/$100 each | Discounter | $49 |
| 100 shares/$100 each | Deep-discounter | $24.99 |

| 500 shares/$30 each | Full-service | $314 |
| 500 shares/$30 each | Discounter | $97 |
| 500 shares/$30 each | Deep-discounter | $25 |

Don't be afraid to ask whichever broker you choose to work with for a commission schedule, and don't think twice about asking for a discount. You'll also want to discuss rates with your broker on a regular basis.

## EDUCATE YOURSELF

Teaching yourself about investing will go a long way toward helping you deal with risk. You can pick up the basics by taking a personal finance course at a local community college or attending an investment seminar sponsored by a nonpartisan group like the American Association of Individual Investors in Chicago (312-280-0170) or the National Center for Women and Retirement Research (800-426-7386). Major mutual fund companies and brokerages now offer retirement planning booklets through their 800 numbers and Internet Web pages as well. The more you understand about the world of investing, the more confident and comfortable you will become with your investment choices.

## JOIN AN INVESTMENT CLUB

You can also learn the ropes and have some fun at the same time by joining an investment club. Of the estimated 50,000 clubs now in operation, 35 percent are female-only, up from 25 percent three years ago. The women-only clubs outperformed men's clubs in nine of the last 13 years. Usually assembled from co-workers or friends, the clubs typically meet monthly at a member's home, the office, or a local library and require monthly cash contributions of anywhere from $25 to $50.

*tip*   To learn more about starting an investment club, write to the National Association of Investors Corp., P.O. Box 220, Royal Oak, Michigan 48068.

In this lesson, you learned a couple of easy ways to bone up on investing strategies and ways to save money buying stocks. In the next lesson, you will view some model investment allocation plans.

# 10

# Putting Together Your Portfolio

*In this lesson, you'll learn the benefits of regular saving and how to determine which investment allocation plan is best for your age and needs. You will also learn the importance of rebalancing your portfolio to help you reach your goals.*

## Balancing Your Portfolio

Now that you know what your investment choices are, it's time to figure out the best mix of investments for your age. In general, the younger you are the more risk you must take to reap the benefits of compounding. While it's important to invest in individual stocks, for many of you, buying shares in mutual funds is the easiest and least volatile way to create a well-balanced portfolio. If you're able to tolerate some risk, try to put up to 8 percent of your savings in individual stocks.

The following table shows how someone who is 25 years old might want to balance her investment portfolio to maximize her returns. The annual average return for this type of invest-ment portfolio is about 12.8 percent.

### RECOMMENDED ASSET ALLOCATION FOR PERSON AGE 25

| | |
|---|---|
| Large-company stock funds | 40% |
| Small-company stock funds | 35% |
| International stock funds | 20% |
| CDs or money market funds | 5% |

The following table shows how someone who is 45 years old might want to divide her investments. The average return for this type of portfolio is about 12.1 percent.

### RECOMMENDED ASSET ALLOCATION FOR PERSON AGE 45

| | |
|---|---|
| Large-company stock funds | 35% |
| Small-company stock funds | 25% |
| International stock funds | 15% |
| Bonds | 20% |
| CDs or money market funds | 5% |

The following table shows how someone who is 65 years old might split up her investments. The average annual return is about 10.6 percent.

### RECOMMENDED ASSET ALLOCATION FOR PERSON AGE 65

| | |
|---|---|
| Large-company stock funds | 20% |
| Small-company stock funds | 10% |
| International stock funds | 10% |
| Bonds | 45% |
| CDs or money market funds | 15% |

Let's look at an example of how a woman who starts early and is willing to take on some risk can balance her 401(k) retirement portfolio for the long run. Susan is 27, and she wants to retire when she is 67. Her current annual income is $40,000. This example assumes she stashes away five percent of her income each year, her employer contributes $1 for every $4 she contributes, and she gets a 3 percent salary raise each year. Her best plan would be to invest the biggest chunk of her savings in global stock funds (45 percent), then put 35 percent of her sum in small-company stock funds and another 20 percent in bond funds. The risk level is high, but the expected annual report would be about 13 percent. Given that scenario, her nest egg would be valued at $3.6 million at retirement.

## THE IMPORTANCE OF REBALANCING

It's a simple investing truth that portfolio balances are thrown off by economic forces. That's because in some years the stock market is roaring and the bond market is declining. Other years, it's the reverse. The best way to keep in line with your goals is to rebalance at least once a year. For example, assume you want to have 70 percent of your retirement money in stock funds and 30 percent in bond funds. Last year, the average stock mutual fund was up 30 percent while the average government bond fund was up just 17 percent. So if you had $70,000 in stock funds and $30,000 in bond funds in January of 1995, by year-end you would have $91,000 in stocks and $35,100 in bonds. That's 72 percent of your money in stocks and 28 percent in bonds. So you would want to sell $2,700 of your stock funds and add that to your bond funds. Moreover, as you grow older you will want to shift your investments gradually to less risky investments, such as bonds or Treasuries.

**Consider Dollar Cost Averaging**   With dollar cost averaging, you set aside a specific amount of money on a regular schedule, say $200, to be invested in the same fund or stock every month. Making small, consistent contributions to your retirement fund helps you control your risk. With this investment strategy, you buy some mutual fund shares, for instance, when they are high-priced and some when they are low-priced. You no longer have the frustration of trying to time your investment to buy low. Moreover, you set a course for regular investing that is critical to building a future nest egg. When investing for retirement becomes a habit, you don't fret over it as much.

# THE MAGIC OF REGULAR SAVINGS

If you invest $200 a month, over time the compounding growth is explosive, as shown in the following table.

### GROWTH OF A $200 PER MONTH INVESTMENT

| YEARS OF INVESTING | 8 PERCENT ANNUAL GROWTH | 10 PERCENT ANNUAL GROWTH |
| --- | --- | --- |
| 5 | $14,800 | $15,620 |
| 10 | $36,840 | $41,320 |
| 20 | $118,580 | $153,140 |

In this lesson, you learned how to allocate your retirement investments to reach the maximum return possible and the importance of regular investing. In the next lesson, you will learn how to accumulate money for your retirement if you have changed jobs frequently and spent time outside the workplace.

# **11**

# **HOW CHANGING JOBS IMPACTS YOUR RETIREMENT**

*In this lesson, you'll learn how to keep your retirement benefits growing and working for you when you switch employers or stop working to raise a family or care for an aging relative.*

## **WHY JOB-JUMPING CAN HURT YOUR RETIREMENT SAVINGS**

The Bureau of Labor Statistics reports that women over 25 stay with an employer an average of 4.8 years, compared to 6.6 years for men. That's just a few months short of the five years typically required for you to qualify for a pension or receive an employer's contributions to a 401(k) plan. The loss can be substantial. For example, you're 45 years old and have been with your current employer for four years and nine months. You're offered a position with a better title and a bigger salary. You'd be foolish to turn it down, right?

Think again. By changing jobs just three months shy of vesting, you could forfeit thousands of dollars that your employers have already contributed to your 401(k).

Before you change jobs, you should do the following:

- Get an updated statement of your accumulated retirement benefits.

- Compare your benefits to your potential new employer's salary offer and retirement plan benefits.

- Ask your current employer whether you're already vested or when you will become vested in your plan. If you change jobs before you are vested, you may lose some or all of your retirement benefits. In many cases, you will only get back the contributions you put in, plus interest.

- Ask your new employer to increase your starting salary to help offset some of those lost retirement benefits.

If you're seriously considering taking the new job, consider these strategies:

- Negotiate for a one-time signing bonus. Invest that sum directly into a tax-deferred account, so that it will continue to grow tax-deferred until retirement rolls around.

- Don't cash out. To avoid income taxes as well as an additional 10 percent penalty, you should roll over your retirement distribution into an IRA or your new employer's plan within 60 days of the time you receive it. You're exempt from paying the penalty if you are $59\frac{1}{2}$ or disabled.

- Even if you know you will need the money to live while you are between jobs, or even if you are moving right to a new employer, have your old employer transfer the money into your new employer's plan, an IRA, or another tax-deferred account. Most employers, however, don't allow new employees to participate in a 401(k) plan for six months or a full year after they begin work. For those who will need the money to live on between jobs, you will be able to slowly withdraw as you need the cash so the penalty and taxes are levied only on the amount you must use.

- If you are already vested, find out what your payment options on your vested retirement benefits are before you leave your old job. Some employers will not let you withdraw the funds until you reach retirement age under their plan. If that's the case, be diligent about letting your old plan administrator know your correct address and telephone number until you can cash out at retirement. Make sure you ask if there are any extra management fees charged to former employers who leave money in a plan.

# The Trouble with Taking Time Off from the Workplace

The stark reality is that women are out of the workforce more than men. The number of years a working woman might have left at age 25 is far less than a man of the same age, as shown in the following table.

| AGE/SEX | PERCENTAGE OF REMAINING LIFE WORKING |
|---------|--------------------------------------|
| 25/Man | 70% |
| 25/Woman | 44% |

*Source: The Department of Labor*

# THE FINANCIAL IMPLICATIONS

Staying out of the workforce for just seven years during a 40-year career may cut your retirement benefits in half. You also lose more than salary and retirement benefits when you aren't on a payroll. You also lose seniority that leads to promotions and pay raises.

Fortunately, there are some measures that will help you overcome these disadvantages.

You should consider working at least part-time, or on a consulting basis. That way you can maintain some visibility and maybe continue to accrue some benefits too. You'll want to be sure to find out what your employer's break in service rules are.

 **Break in Service**   A break in service is defined as not completing at least 500 hours per year in paid status. If you work less than 500 hours, when you return to work, your vesting clock may start all over again.

If you are taking a pregnancy or adoption leave, up to 501 hours will be counted as service and not a break in service, so the leave will not reduce your benefits.

Thanks to the passage of the Family and Medical Leave Act in 1993, you may not have to miss out on benefits while you are out caring for an ailing parent or relative. Companies must now offer some form of eldercare, as well as child care benefits in the form of paid or unpaid leave for up to 12 weeks, as well as a tax break. Typically, if your elderly parent lives with you and is disabled and unable to care for him or herself, your employer will offer a dependent care spending account. Many of these plans let you use pre-tax dollars up to a limit of $5,000 to put towards paying for care.

There's also now a tax break for workers who must pay to hire someone to care for an ailing parent. To offset the costs, you may claim a credit of $480 to $720, depending on your total income and the cost of the care. To learn more about what your employer can do to help you hang on to your benefits when you are forced to care for another person, call your human resources department.

In this lesson, you learned what you can do to combat the devastating financial implications of switching jobs before you are fully vested in a retirement plan. In the next lesson, you will learn how marriage and divorce can influence your retirement benefits and financial security.

# Marriage, Divorce, and Retirement Planning

*In this lesson, you will learn how to receive the most from your husband's retirement benefits and your own plan during your marriage and what to do if you get a divorce.*

## Plan to Be Alone

If you are married, you should manage all your finances as if you were going to be alone one day. Of course, you hope your marriage will be long and happy; however, you should bear in mind the following depressing statistics:

- More than 75 percent of people living below the poverty level in this country are women. That's largely because women live longer than men do and frequently run through their financial resources before they die.

- Half of all women married in the past 20 years will eventually divorce, according to the Census Bureau.

- Even if your marriage does last, your spouse is not likely to survive you unless he's years younger or in better health. It is estimated that 90 percent of women will be responsible for their finances at some point in their lives.

# WHAT YOU CAN DO NOW

There are several steps you can take now to make sure you can deal with the sudden loss of your spouse without running into financial trouble.

- Make sure your name is on all household accounts and investments.

- Keep at least one credit card in your name to establish your creditworthiness.

- Consider keeping some money in an investment account in your name only. You'll never forgive yourself if you wake up and find your soon-to-be-ex-husband has emptied your joint accounts.

- Ask your spouse for a detailed account of his employer-provided benefits.

- Find out who is named as beneficiary on all your husband's insurance policies.

- Decide who you want to name as beneficiaries on your own employer-provided retirement plan and IRA.

- If you want a beneficiary other than your spouse on your employer-provided plan, your husband will have to sign a waiver form that your employer can give you. His signature has to be notarized.

- If you have been divorced, your ex-husband might be entitled to some of your benefits, depending on your divorce agreement. Make sure you are clear on just what he might be entitled to and tell your spouse.

- If your husband has been married before, you'll want to find out if under his divorce agreement his ex-wife has any rights to his retirement benefits.

## Consider a Prenuptial Agreement

If you're bringing valuable assets such as property or expensive jewelry, it may make sense to outline your various assets and financial responsibilities in a legally binding prenuptial agreement. You'll have to decide if you want to merge all your assets and liabilities. Moreover, you'll have to determine how to divide property you acquired before and during your marriage in case of a divorce.

## Take Action Before You Divorce

If you've been having marital difficulties or are contemplating divorce, you should talk to an attorney before making any major financial decisions or making any agreements with your spouse, such as selling your house. However, you should be aware of your legal rights under divorce as well as the rules governing benefit plans.

Typically you will be entitled to a portion of any retirement benefits your ex-husband accrued during your marriage. It will help if you can do the following:

- Find out the value of all your husband's retirement benefits from all his past employers and current employer.

- Be sure you are listed as a surviving spouse for each plan. Otherwise, if your ex-husband dies before he reaches retirement, you may receive nothing at all.

- To get a share of his benefits pension, 401(k), or IRA, you'll need a lawyer to petition a state court for a Qualified Domestic Relations Order.

**Qualified Domestic Relations Order (QDRO)**
A QDRO is a state domestic relations court order that requires an employee's retirement plan to be divided between the employee, a spouse, and any children.

- Call the various plan administrators and ask how the plan handles QDROs.

- If you receive a lump sum, roll over the funds directly to an IRA where the money can continue to grow tax-free until you retire.

You don't have to wait to receive the money awarded by the QDRO. An alternative is to get the funds in cash at the settlement of the divorce. Your spouse might opt to give you the cash equivalent from funds outside his retirement plans, but that sum will not be eligible for a tax-free IRA rollover.

**tip**    If you are dividing IRA money, a transfer of funds under a divorce decree is not considered taxable. The assets are treated as if a new IRA has been set up.

# WHAT YOUR QDRO MUST CONTAIN

A QDRO must contain your ex-spouse's name and last known mailing address. Each plan that is covered by the QDRO should be listed with its correct name. In addition, it should list the name and address of alternate payees. That is normally you, but could also be a child. It should clearly state the total amount of money or precise percentage of your ex-husband's benefits to be paid to the alternative payees. A QDRO should also explain the method the plan administrator used to determine the sum to be paid. Finally, make sure it spells out the exact number of payments.

# TIME YOUR DIVORCE

It may pay to time your divorce. You can qualify for Social Security benefits based on your ex-husband's earnings when you both reach age 62, even if he has remarried, hasn't retired, or hasn't begun to receive benefits himself. To do so, however, you must have been married for at least 10 years and you must not have remarried. So if you're thinking of splitting up after nine and one-half years, you'd be well served if you can stick it out for just a bit longer.

In this lesson, you learned how to manage your finances during a marriage and during divorce. In the next lesson, you will learn why long-term health insurance might keep your retirement funds from eroding as you grow older.

# The Toll of Medical Expenses

*In this lesson, you'll learn how to shop for long-term care insurance to help you avoid using your retirement savings to pay for medical bills.*

## Health Care for Seniors

Roughly 80 percent of widows now living in poverty were not poor before their husbands died, according to the General Accounting Office. Most of the couple's savings were eroded because they were used to pay for the husband's medical expenses. If you plan ahead of time and select the right health insurance, you can avoid this situation.

## Taking Advantage of Medicare

At age 65, providing you are eligible for Social Security or can claim benefits on your spouse's or ex-spouse's account, you can automatically enroll in Medicare, the national insurance program for seniors. You apply for Medicare through your local Social Security office. To make certain you get coverage immediately with the lowest premiums, it's a good idea to enroll three months before your actual birthday. If you wait until after your birthday, you may wind up paying premiums that are 10 percent higher.

Medicare consists of two parts:

- The first portion is free and covers hospitalization, including nursing care and some home health care. Because there is no charge, there is no reason not to sign up for this coverage. Even if you have other health insurance from your employer, Medicare will pick up your plan's deductibles.

- The second part, which covers basic medical insurance from doctors' services to outpatient surgery, medical supplies, and some prescription drugs, is optional. To receive benefits for this second part, you must pay a monthly premium of around $40, which is deducted automatically from your Social Security check. At that cost, even if you are still covered by a company plan, this will pay for your deductibles.

You may mistakenly assume that Medicare is a broad program that covers most of your medical expenses. In fact, Medicare is far narrower than you think. Medicare does not cover the following:

- A deductible of approximately $700 when you enter a hospital

- A portion of the costs if you stay in the hospital more than 60 days

- Private rooms or private nurses

- Only a small part of the cost of the services of a skilled nurse

- Fees for annual physical exams, hearing aids, basic dental care, or eyeglasses

- Most medical expenses incurred when you are traveling outside North America

For the medical portion of Medicare, you will pay a $100 annual deductible and 20 percent of the Medicare-approved expenses.

# MEDICARE SUPPLEMENT POLICIES

Because Medicare is not a total health insurance plan, you'll probably want to add some extra insurance, called a Medicare supplement policy, or a Medigap policy. A basic Medigap policy covers:

- An additional 365 days of hospitalization

- The 20 percent of medical expenses that Medicare doesn't cover

- The first three pints of blood you use each year

You pay a monthly premium for Medigap coverage, but this amount varies widely by state. In Florida, for example, you'd pay $80 per month with most companies, so shop around for the best price from a reputable company. You can increase coverage for an extra fee. You should sign-up for a Medigap policy that covers hospital deductibles, foreign travel emergency care, annual physical and eye exams, and prescription drugs of up to $3,000 annually. To get all this coverage, you could pay more than three times the cost of a basic Medigap policy.

Medicare Select is available in some states. This program provides an alternative to the standard Medicare supplement. The Medicare beneficiary enrolls in an HMO and gets much more than basic Medicare coverage at no additional charge. The downside is typical of any managed care program—you may not be comfortable with the physicians in the HMO.

## FINDING OUT MORE ABOUT MEDICARE AND MEDIGAP POLICIES

There are several places you can contact to learn more about these policies:

- Your local Social Security office will have brochures and information about all the current rules.

- You can order *The Medicare Handbook* from the Social Security Administration by calling 800-772-1213.

- The American Association for Retired Persons (AARP) publishes a free booklet *Medigap: A Consumer's Guide.* Write AARP, 601 E Street NW, Washington, DC 20049.

- Your state insurance or health department will also have information about Medigap policies.

## LONG-TERM CARE INSURANCE

As you and your husband approach age 50, you should begin to look into long-term care insurance, which picks up the tab for nursing home care. Today, more than 130 insurance companies sell individual long-term care policies. Because nursing home costs can average $40,000 annually, without the proper insurance to pay the bills, your retirement savings could be easily depleted. The key is to buy the extra coverage before you hit retirement age. The younger you are when you start paying for this insurance, the cheaper it will be. A 50-year-old woman will pay about 60 percent less than a 65-year-old for the identical coverage.

It's naive to think you might never need this kind of health care. A 65-year-old woman has a 40 percent chance of spending at least one day in a nursing home, a 20 percent chance of spending a year there, and a 10 percent chance of spending five or more years in a nursing home, according to the New England Journal of Medicine. In addition, the American Association of Retired Persons estimates that in the next decade, nearly two-thirds of the seniors using nursing homes will be women.

## What Long-Term Care Policies Cover

The policy benefits usually cover the cost of nursing home care or for care in your own home. Typically, the most affordable policies allow for $100 per day care expenses. The sum does adjust with inflation. Moreover, benefits usually don't start until after a three month waiting period and will last less than five years. You can, however, find policies with shorter waiting periods and longer periods of coverage, but your costs will skyrocket. In fact, it's not unusual for premiums to double.

# WHAT DOES LONG-TERM INSURANCE COST?

The premium for a married, 50-year-old woman can be as low as $500 per year. That same policy for a 65-year-old might cost $1,000 per year. The key is to buy a policy while you are still healthy and young, say, age 55.

# FINDING A POLICY

You can obtain a free list of companies that offer long-term care insurance policies by writing to Health Insurance Association of America, 555 13th Street NW, Washington, DC 20004.

 **tip** The National Association of Insurance Commissioners also publishes a guide to long-term insurance and includes some recommendations. For a free copy, write NAIC, 120 West 12th Street, Suite 1100, Kansas City, MO 64105.

# WHAT TO LOOK FOR IN A POLICY

Here are the features you should shop for:

- Look for a policy that covers all levels of care from skilled care with a licensed medical professional to basic custodial care that covers basic needs such as feeding.

- A policy should not require a prior hospital stay before the benefits start.

- Make sure the policy guarantees the rates for at least the first five years. Although most companies say the rates are flat for the rest of your life, they do retain the right to bump up the premiums for an entire group of policyholders, for example, people who live in Nebraska.

- You should only buy a policy that will waive all premiums once you enter a nursing home.

- The policy must be guaranteed to be renewable for life.

- You should have a "free look" period that lets you change your mind or cancel the policy at no cost within 30 days.

- Home care should be a regular benefit. The best policies let you switch between nursing home care and home care.

- Make sure the policy specifically covers such disorders as strokes, Alzheimer's disease, or Parkinson's disease.

- Deal only with insurers who are safe and have a high rating. Check a company's safety ratings with A.M. Best (908-439-2200), Duff & Phelps (312-368-3157), Standard & Poor's (212-208-1527), Moody's (212-553-0377), or Weiss Research (800-289-9222) before purchasing a policy.

- Look to large, reliable insurers who regularly write these policies and upgrade their offerings.

- Look for a policy with at least $100 a day in coverage. Some offer as little as $60 a day.

# HOW TO TRIM PREMIUM COSTS

There are many ways to cut the costs of long-term insurance:

- You can opt for a longer elimination period, or deductible period. The elimination period can range from first day coverage to 20 days to 90 days or longer. If you have enough assets to cover the first few months of care before the insurance takes over, you will save on premiums. You can cut your yearly premiums by $100 by raising your deductible from 20 days to 100 days.

- Ask for a spousal discount if you are married. Many insurers will slash your premiums by 10 to 15 percent if both spouses buy a policy. And if the policies have been in effect for at least 10 years, some insurers will waive all premiums after the first spouse dies.

- Check to see if your employer offers group long-term care insurance, which is less expensive than an individual policy.

In this lesson, you learned how you can safeguard your retirement money by signing up for Medicare and Medigap policies and purchasing long-term care insurance for you and your spouse. In the next lesson, you will learn about working after retirement.

# 14

# WORKING BEYOND RETIREMENT

*In this lesson, you'll learn how to evaluate an early retirement offer and how returning to work after retirement can affect your Social Security benefits and taxes.*

## WHAT TO MAKE OF AN EARLY RETIREMENT OFFER

As a result of the increasing corporation downsizing among major employers, more and more companies are offering employees early retirement payouts. The offers vary from employer to employer, but many are attractive offers that might even give you enough capital to jump-start a new career or business.

Some firms offer extended health and life insurance benefits. Others beef up your pension checks by adding five years to your tenure at the company. And some agree to pay you a certain amount of extra income to tide you over until your Social Security benefits start.

If your employer makes an offer, you should ask these questions before accepting or rejecting the offer:

- Will you need to find another job?
- If so, will you be able to find a good job elsewhere?
- Do you have enough saved without siphoning retirement funds to live on until you get another job or start earning income again?
- What will happen to your pension benefits?
- Will the payout be counted as income and taxed accordingly?
- Where will you invest the lump sum to keep it working for you?

## THE CASE FOR WORKING AFTER RETIREMENT

Whether you opt for an early retirement payout or simply retire at the age your employer mandates, you may not want to or be able to afford to retire in your 60s. You might total all your potential Social Security benefits, employer's plan benefits, and personal savings and be stunned to find it simply still isn't enough. Or like many retirees today, you would rather retire to a second career rather than play shuffleboard everyday. But what does all this mean for your retirement plan?

Truthfully, not everyone is ready to retire when the time rolls around, and the option of continuing to work, provided you're in good health, can be financially rewarding. By delaying retirement, you will increase the benefits you receive from

Social Security, from your employer's plan, and of course, your own savings. Then too, chances are if you hang on a few more years, you will get some cost-of-living raises, which in turn boost your future retirement benefits.

Say, for instance, you were born in 1946 and you wait until age 68 to apply for Social Security. You might be able to increase the amount of your Social Security payments by a compounded 26 percent for the rest of your life.

The following table shows how your Social Security check can expand if you wait until age 68 to retire.

| WHEN TO RETIRE | SOCIAL SECURITY PAYOUT |
|---|---|
| Retire at age 65 in 2016 | Social Security pays an estimated $3,200 per month (adjusted for 4 percent annual inflation) |
| Retire at age 68 in 2019 | Social Security pays an estimated $4,000 per month (adjusted for 4 percent annual inflation) |

# DELAY APPLYING FOR SOCIAL SECURITY

The federal government really wants to entice you to work past retirement age. If you stay on the job past age 65 and continue contributing to the Social Security Administration, you'll get an extra retirement credit of 3 percent a year up until age 70, when you actually retire. The percentage is slowly increasing, and by the year 2009, the credit bonus will be 8 percent.

It's a guaranteed return that compounds annually and is partially tax-free. And if your income gets bumped up in the meantime, even better.

The following table shows how the bonus for retiring past age 65 works.

| BIRTH YEAR | YEARLY BONUS |
| --- | --- |
| 1935–1936 | 6.0% |
| 1937–1938 | 6.5% |
| 1939–1940 | 7.0% |
| 1941–1942 | 7.5% |
| 1943 and beyond | 8.0% |

Your pot gets bigger because your benefits are calculated on how much you earn. And no one says that you actually have to stay in the workforce. You can retire at 65, but not apply for Social Security for a couple of years. Each year you wait your bonus kicks in, and of course, that's a lifetime benefit. (Like Medicare, Social Security is not automatic; you must apply for it.)

## PARTIAL RETIREMENT

Nearly one-quarter of full-time workers now return to the workplace after officially retiring. Some firms even rehire retirees on a part-time basis.

# How to Find Part-Time Work

While you may not be able to find a job that perfectly matches your experience or your needs, more and more so-called retirees are returning to the workforce. In fact, many employers welcome older employees because of their experience and maturity in the workforce. Try some of the following strategies if you want to go back to work:

- Check with your company to see if it has a flexible retirement option.

- Contact the Senior Career Planning & Placement Service, 257 Park Avenue, New York, NY 10010, (212-529-6660). This group, a division of the National Executive Service Corps, places retired executives in part-time positions around the country.

- Temporary agencies also offer a range of positions for older workers. Two agencies are Kelly Services and Adia Services, with offices across the country.

- Look into Operation ABLE (Ability Based on Long Experience), an agency for senior-employment programs. This not-for-profit organization assists with job searches and matches. For more information, call the hotline at 312-782-3335, or write Operation ABLE, 180 North Wabash Ave., Chicago, IL 60601.

# Starting Your Own Business

You might even want to start your own small business after retirement. You set your own hours, go at your own pace, and hopefully do something you love. Don't, however, sacrifice your retirement savings to bankroll this venture.

**tip**

To learn more about starting your own business, call the Service Corps of Retired Executives (SCORE), which is administered by the U.S. Small Business Administration. There are more than 750 SCORE locations across the country. They sponsor workshops and seminars, and can provide valuable advice on starting a business after retirement.

There are also dozens of books on how to start your own business in retirement, including the *100 Best Retirement Businesses* by Lisa Angowski Rogak (Upstart Publishing, $15.95), and *Starting a Mini-Business: A Guide Book for Seniors* by Nancy Olsen (Fair Oaks Publishing, $6.95).

## WORKING AND SOCIAL SECURITY

If you work and collect Social Security after age 65, Uncle Sam will gladly tax you 33 1/3 percent on top of your regular income taxes. In other words, the government takes back $1 for every $3 you earn over a certain earned-income limit which changes annually. The Social Security ceiling this year is $12,500 and will increase gradually to $30,000 in the year 2002. But after you reach 70, you can earn as much as you like and still collect full Social Security benefits.

In this lesson, you learned how to find work after you retire and what the impact those extra earning years can have on your Social Security payout. In the next lesson, you will learn how you can tap the equity you've built up in your home as another source of extra retirement income.

# 15

# TAPPING INTO YOUR HOME EQUITY

*In this lesson, you'll learn how tapping into the equity in your home can provide extra cash during your retirement.*

Even if you've carefully planned your retirement, you may find yourself strapped after you actually retire and are faced with unexpected medical and other living expenses. There are a couple of ways you can use your home to help you bump up your available cash.

## HOME EQUITY LINES OF CREDIT

A *home equity loan* is a loan that lets you borrow against the value of your home, minus any outstanding mortgage. In some cases, you get a check for the full amount of the loan, but usually, you have access to a line of credit for the amount of the home equity loan and can write checks as needed.

These loans are usually limited to 75 to 80 percent of the current value of your home minus the balance on your mortgage. The advantage of home equity loans is that the interest you pay on the funds is deductible. Most lenders today will waive processing and closing fees and even take applications over the phone. Approvals can be made in less than an hour. Rates vary from region to region and can range from as low as 7 percent to as high as 12 percent. There are, of course, teaser rates that dip as low as 4 percent, but to qualify you must borrow a minimum amount ranging from $5,000 to $20,000. And those rates usually expire after three to six months. After that they fluctuate monthly based on the prime rate plus one to three percentage points.

# Reverse Mortgages

A *reverse mortgage* is an arrangement whereby a bank pays you a set amount per month based on the amount of equity built up in your home.

To apply for a reverse mortgage, you must be over age 62 and your home must be owned without a mortgage, or just a small one. The lender pays you, the homeowner, a monthly sum for a set term of years based on your total equity in the house. You continue to hold the title to the house and are responsible for its upkeep. When you sell your house or die, the amount you were loaned via the monthly payments, plus interest, is then repaid to the lender from the proceeds of the sale of the house. The amount you can borrow depends on your current age, the market value of your home, and prevailing interest rates.

## When Should You Consider a Reverse Mortgage?

This is one source of income you should wait to use. The older you are when you apply, the more funds you'll be able to get.

The classic reverse mortgage borrower is a widow in her mid-70s and the mortgage might pay around $400 a month.

You should be aware that some reverse mortgages pay women a lower monthly payment than they would a man, even if the house is worth the same amount. That's because of your longer life expectancy.

Reverse mortgages guaranteed by the Federal Housing Authority (FHA) are not allowed to use this gender bias. Moreover, these government-backed loans guarantee that if you die owing more than the home is worth, the lender can't go after your heirs or other assets to pay off the loan. FHA-backed loans are limited to a maximum of $124,875 in good urban neighborhoods. You can call your local U.S. Housing and Urban Development office for details about FHA lenders in your city, or call 800-732-6643.

## HOW ARE REVERSE MORTGAGES STRUCTURED?

Reverse mortgages are set up in one of three ways:

- *The line of credit plan.* This flexible option lets you obtain a line of credit, which increases as you grow older. You can tap the money any time you feel like it.

- *The tenure plan.* This way you get a fixed monthly loan for as long as you stay in your home. The FHA only insures this type of reverse mortgage.

- *The term plan.* You can choose how many years of payments you want. The shorter the term, obviously, the higher the monthly payment. At the end of the time period, you stop getting payments, but don't have to repay the loan until you sell the house.

# THE DRAWBACKS OF REVERSE MORTGAGES

There are some disadvantages to reverse mortgages. These mortgages have a bad reputation for charging onerous up-front costs and carry relatively high interest rates—sometimes higher than 20 percent in the early years because of those high upfront fees. Even after, for example, seven years, if your home is valued at $150,000 and you signed up at age 75, your rate could still be nearly 17 percent. You'll pay normal closing costs, usually one percent of your home's value, plus an insurance premium of about 2 percent of the home's value. If you are not planning to stay put for several years, it won't benefit you to go for one. And if there is not a provision for rising property values, you might lose the appreciation of the value of your home.

The following table shows how the maximum monthly payments for a reverse mortgage might work.

| AGE | $50,000 HOUSE | $75,000 HOUSE | $100,000 HOUSE |
|---|---|---|---|
| *An FHA-insured plan: payment for life* | | | |
| 65 | $90 | $162 | $234 |
| 75 | $154 | $259 | $364 |
| 85 | $272 | $438 | $604 |
| | | | |
| *A 10-year term* | | | |
| 65 | $146 | $262 | $378 |
| 75 | $233 | $391 | $549 |
| 85 | $340 | $547 | $755 |

*Source: Federal National Mortgage Association*

## LEARNING MORE ABOUT REVERSE MORTGAGES

There are four reverse mortgage programs that dominate the industry:

- The Department of Housing and Urban Development's Home Equity Conversion Mortgage (HECM) (1-202-708-1422; or HUD office nearest you)
- Fannie Mae's "Homekeeper" (1-800-732-6643)
- Household Bank's Household program (1-800-233-0542)
- TransAmerica Corp.'s Home First plan (1-800-538-5569)

**tip** For more information about reverse mortgages, write to the National Center for Home Equity Conversion, a not-for-profit company, at 1210 East College Drive, Suite 300, Marshall, MN 56358.

The AARP Home Equity Information Center provides detailed reports on reverse mortgages, including an honest look at the risks and benefits. Write to the Consumer Affairs Section, AARP, 601 E. Street NW, Washington, DC 20049.

## OTHER HOUSING ALTERNATIVES

You could sell your home outright and move to a community where the living expenses are cheaper. By doing so, you can take advantage of a once-in-a-lifetime tax bonus. You will not have to pay federal tax on up to $125,000 of profit from the sale of your home if either you or your spouse is over age 55 when the house is sold. You may still be required to pay state tax. You must also have lived in your house as a principal residence for three of the five years before the sale.

There are several books that can help you locate potential retirement areas that can offer a higher quality of life for less. One good source is *Fabulous Places to Retire in America* by Lee and Laralee Rosenberg (Career Press, $14.95).

Tax information may help you decide where to strike off for. Not all states tax your pension income. Fifteen states tax Social Security benefits, and other locales levy no state or local taxes. Florida and Nevada, for instance, have no state income tax.

## STAYING PUT

You can't stand the thought of moving, but you're house rich and cash poor. One option is to rent out a room—set aside a finished basement or an entire floor of the house for a renter. You'll probably pay tax on the income and have some landlord headaches, but it will generate some needed cash.

Another option is to sell your home, but then sign a lease-back agreement. This allows you to continue living in your home, but you'll now pay a monthly rental fee. These arrangements can be hard to nail down, and often are made between children and parents, but in the right circumstances, both parties can benefit.

In this lesson, you learned how you can use your home to help you get through periods of low cash flow and bump up your monthly income during your retirement. In the next lesson, you will learn the basics of life insurance and disability insurance and how they fit into your retirement plan.

# 16

# LOOKING INTO LIFE AND DISABILITY INSURANCE

*In this lesson, you will learn the role life insurance and disability insurance play in the retirement planning process.*

## LIFE INSURANCE AS A RETIREMENT TOOL

Buying life insurance is enough to make your head spin, and on the surface, seems to be one of the most complex financial decisions you'll have to confront. But the basics of life insurance are not that hard to understand.

The first question you need to ask yourself is do you really need it? In many cases, putting your money into a top-flight mutual fund, instead of an insurance policy, is a far better way to invest for retirement.

You don't need life insurance if:

- You are under 30, single, and have no dependents.

- You are married with no children and you both work full-time.

- You are nearing or are already retired. Your children are on their own and your spouse is not dependent on your income.

You do need life insurance if:

- You are a working parent and your children are dependent on your income.

- You are a stay-at-home mom and your contribution would be difficult or too expensive to replace.

- You are in business for yourself or with a partner and want to leave money for your heirs to buy out your partner or pay taxes.

If you need insurance, the key issue becomes how much coverage you should get. This is perhaps the toughest sum to compute. There are many factors that have to be included in the equation. Review the following issues:

- If you have kids, how much would your husband need to pay for child care?

- How many years would it take your husband to replace your income?

- How long until he might remarry and have another wage-earner to replace your lost income?

- If you are a single mother, how long will your children need your financial support?

- Will your children need money to pay for college? If so, how much will they need?

## CALCULATING THE AMOUNT OF LIFE INSURANCE YOU NEED

Answer the following questions to determine the dollar amount of life insurance you need to buy:

1. What is your annual budget? $_____

2. What is your projected budget in five years? (Keep in mind the inflation rate.) $_____

3. What is the percentage your income contributes to the overall budget? _____%

Your contribution multiplied by the annual budget multiplied by five years is how much life insurance you might need. $_____

## WHAT KIND OF INSURANCE SHOULD YOU BUY?

There are two types of life insurance you can buy. *Term insurance* is the simplest, most affordable kind of life insurance to purchase when you are planning to insure yourself for at least 20 years. You pay an annual guaranteed premium based on your age, health, the insurer's cost of paying agent commissions and mailings to you, and how much the insurer thinks they can earn by investing your money until you die.

**Term Insurance**   Term insurance is insurance that pays a specific death benefit to your survivors.

The other type of insurance you can buy is *cash-value life insurance*. There are several variations of cash-value policies; the most common are whole life, universal life, and variable life.

**Cash-Value Insurance**   Cash-value policies are a combined life policy and savings plan.

With whole life insurance, you get a traditional death benefit. Your money is invested primarily in bonds and you get a fixed modest return. With universal policies, you can adjust both your premium and death benefit according to your needs and circumstances.

With a variable life policy, your money is invested in your choice of stocks, bonds, or money-market funds. The money you put in grows tax-deferred, like an IRA. A percentage of that money goes toward your yearly premiums. The lion's share, however, goes into savings investments that accumulate tax-free as long as you live. In most cases, the premium is fixed, and the insurer pays an agreed-on benefit when you die. Over time, the money that accumulates can be pulled out for retirement income.

# WHO SHOULD CONSIDER A CASH-VALUE POLICY?

Women who earn more than $100,000 annually and want more than $700,000 in coverage might shop for a cash-value policy. This policy is also a good option if you have contributed the maximum to an IRA and 401(k) plan and want another tax-deferred savings plan.

**tip**

It can take almost a decade for you to actually have a valuable investment due to the toll that fees and commissions take. Moreover, it's tricky to estimate what the cash value of your policy will really be worth 15 years down the road. It all depends on the actual dividends that are paid out by your insurer, not what they project when you sign up.

# WITHDRAWING THE MONEY

To withdraw your funds, you can borrow, without tax penalty, against the policy's cash value without losing any insurance benefit. You must pay it back, or when you die the funds borrowed are paid by what's left of the policy. You can also give up or surrender your policy completely and receive the total cash value sum. What you paid in premiums over the years is tax-free, the rest is taxable.

# SHOPPING FOR TERM INSURANCE

When you're comparing policies, you should evaluate the terms of the policies carefully. Among the factors you should consider:

- Do you want premiums that increase annually or premiums with a set term that remains the same for five to fifteen years? If you opt for the fixed premiums, which are very popular, make sure that you agree to guaranteed premiums, not projected premiums. Guaranteed policies may cost more, but they are worth it.

- If you pick a ten-year policy, keep it for the entire time period. Most people cancel term policies after seven years on average.

- Do you want a guaranteed annual renewable term policy or a reentry policy? The renewable insurance policy does not require you to take a medical exam annually. With reentry policies, you must requalify each year, and you probably have to pick up the $400 plus cost of that exam.

- Do you want the option to convert to a cash-value policy down the road? Again, it usually costs more, but if you take this path, you can forego another medical exam.

- What age do you want the policy to expire? Many term policies expire at age 70.

# TRACKING DOWN THE BEST PRICE ON A POLICY

**tip** Contact a quote service company that mails you quotes on five of the best-priced policies that fit your needs. There's usually not a charge for the quotes, and typically you can buy the policy from the quote service firm, but you don't have to. Also check insurers' safety ratings.

- Insurance Quote Services Inc. (800-972-1104)
- SelectQuote (800-343-1985)
- TermQuote (800-444-8376)
- Quotesmith Corp. (800-556-9393)

Be sure to buy only from an insurer with the highest safety rankings from independent evaluators such as: A.M. Best (900-555-2378), Duff & Phelps (312-368-3157), Moody's Investors Service (212-553-0377), Standard & Poor's (212-208-1527), and Weiss Research (800-289-9222). Weiss charges you $15 for a report on a company over the phone. Best charges $4.95 for each rating, plus the cost of the call. The other companies provide one rating at no cost.

# SHOPPING FOR CASH-VALUE POLICIES

Keep a clear head during the sales pitch. You'll be inundated with charts full of column after column dotted with numbers and a plethora of projections, including ages, years, values, and benefits. Avoid policies that in the first few years list under the "Surrender Value" column an amount of zero. That means the insurer and your agent are pocketing your premiums in commissions and other perks. Look for discount brokers who offer low-load insurance. Commissions can be as much as 50 percent cheaper.

*tip* Seek out firms that sell directly to you without an agent acting as middleman, such as USAA Life (800-531-8000) or Ameritas (800-552-3553). For more information, contact the National Insurance Consumer Organization (NICO) at 121 N. Payne Street, Alexandria, VA 22314.

## DON'T IGNORE DISABILITY INSURANCE

For most of you the chances of being disabled are far greater than the chances of dying. A serious injury from a car accident or critical illness can wipe out all your retirement savings before you know it. Disability insurance can provide some cushion. Most large employers provide some type of disability coverage, but two-thirds of U.S. companies don't. Some states, including California and New York, require companies to offer short-term disability benefits that might last around six months. Find out from your benefits department exactly what your employer offers, sometimes it can run as high as a year of disability pay, but usually it is a far shorter time span. Most employer plans cover you for 60 percent of your salary. If you leave the firm to go out on your own for some reason, you'll have to get your own policy, which can be difficult if you have any health problems. Look into adding to your existing policy with an independent one that doesn't duplicate the coverage you already have.

The biggest problem with disability insurance is that it is expensive to buy, and for women it is even more costly. Many insurers are now raising women's premiums as much as 50 percent because they have found that women file more claims than men do. It might cost a 45-year-old woman, earning around $45,000, about $700 a year for a policy that starts after she's been out of work for six months and pays out $2,000 monthly.

## COST-SAVING TIPS

There are several strategies that you can use to reduce the cost of disability insurance. Use the following guidelines to lower your premiums:

- The longer the waiting period for benefits, the less you pay in premiums.

- Comparison shop with at least two insurers, but remember to compare the exact coverage from company to company.

- Check safety ratings. This won't lower your premium, but it will protect you from losing what you've paid in premiums should your insurer fail.

In this lesson, you learned how life insurance and disability insurance can protect your retirement nest egg. In the next lesson, you'll learn some estate planning tips involving trusts that can play an important part in your overall retirement plan.

# 17

# ESTATE PLANNING AND TRUSTS

*In this lesson, you'll learn why trusts and general estate planning are an important part of your retirement planning.*

## THE LIVING TRUST

When you're young and your career is proceeding smoothly, it's hard to imagine that one day more than likely you'll be unable to deal with your own finances.

A *living trust* can give you professional management of all or a portion of your assets during your lifetime. It's a method of holding title to your assets, such as the title of your house. It doesn't involve more taxes, and you still retain complete control. But should you become unable to handle your own affairs due to an illness or accident, you can rest assured that a reliable person will handle these things for you. While you are named the trustee, or you and your husband co-trustees, you also name a successor trustee to take over if you are unable to manage your affairs. That person can then legally manage your financial affairs while you are incapacitated.

There are two advantages to having a living trust:

- It allows your heirs to skip the hassle of passing your assets through the probate process on your death. Probate, a public court process, can take up to two years to legally change the asset titles to the heirs. Probate legal fees can run as high as 10 percent of your estate's total assets.

- It is revocable, meaning that you can change the provisions of the trust, such as renaming a trustee or even terminating the trust.

You should consult an experienced estate planning attorney to handle the legal documents and necessary paperwork to create a living trust. You will have to rename all your assets in the trust name, say, Sandy Jones Trust or Sandy and Tom Jones Trust. That includes any CDs, your house, money market accounts, mutual funds, and any other investment accounts.

To do this, you write a notice to the bank or mutual fund and send along a certified copy of the first and last pages of the trust documents and the page that says who has trustee rights. Then, when you write checks on the accounts or buy and sell shares, you simply add the word "trustee" after your name.

Your other choice is to draw up what is known as a durable power of attorney. Many states allow you to have a durable power of attorney, which will continue even if you are incapacitated. If this is permitted in your state, it may give you similar benefits as a living trust and cost far less.

## How a Marital Trust Works

A *marital trust* can be established as a type of living trust that will manage an estate and pay out income to a surviving spouse. It can be a good way to divvy up assets should this be a second or third marriage for you because it allows you to say who gets your assets after you and your spouse die. If you are getting married late in life, and you and your husband have a sizable estate, this would allow you to execute a trust that will pay the surviving spouse income, and then the principal can go to your children.

## How an Irrevocable Trust Works

Instead of handing over a sum of cash directly to your children or grandchildren, you can establish an *irrevocable trust* and name the recipient as the beneficiary. A good place to put the money is in a no-load mutual fund that is set up specifically for irrevocable trust accounts and invest in long-term growth vehicles. Most fund families now offer these. These funds have minimums that start around $250. The fund might require gifts to children to remain in the fund for at least a decade or until the child reaches a certain age. The advantages to you are that you can reduce your taxable assets and you can still invest the assets yourself. However, you can't tap into the fund for your personal use.

 **A Gift to an Irrevocable Trust** This is a method of giving away up to $10,000 per year per child or grandchild with no tax penalty.

## How to Pick a Trustee

This is a difficult task for most people. A trustee can be a person, say, your attorney, or an institution such as your local bank. In either case, you'll pay an annual fee (regulated by state law) for their services, which is usually a percentage of the trust's assets. Unlike an executor of your estate, who is only responsible for dividing up your estate's assets to the beneficiaries named in your will, a trustee usually must continue to manage the fund in the trust for the duration of the trust. That means they must be able to continually invest the money in a safe, responsible manner.

The pros of selecting a bank to handle this for you is that a bank will last for as long as you need its services and an individual might not. A bank can usually provide you with more computerized services, and you usually have an entire team working for you—an investment officer, a tax planner, and a trust officer to work with your beneficiaries.

Nonetheless, a bank's trust department can be a pretty cold and impersonal place. One way to get around this is to name a co-trustee, such as your husband or your sister, and give that person the power to switch trustees.

## How to Execute a Trust

You'll need to find a local attorney who specializes in trust estate planning. If you have trouble finding one who you feel comfortable with, you might call Estate Planning Specialists, Inc. (800-223-9610). For a fee of about $69, they will give you a custom analysis and recommend estate planning techniques.

In this lesson, you learned several methods of estate planning that involve setting up trust accounts. In the next lesson, you will discover how giving educational gifts to grandchildren and charitable gift-giving can affect your retirement plan.

# **18**

# ESTATE PLANNING AND GIFTS

*In this lesson, you will learn how educational and medical gifts to grandchildren, as well as charitable gifts, can become an integral part of your retirement planning.*

## EDUCATIONAL GIFTS AND MEDICAL GIFTS

Grandparents can give an unlimited sum of money to a grandchild provided the money is spent on education or for medical purposes. This means paying for tuition anywhere from nursery school to graduate school or care for a grandchild. The money, however, must go directly to the institution.

This type of gift is useful as a way to lower your current taxes and pass along money that is free of estate taxes to another generation. Still, this technique is most advantageous if your annual income is roughly $100,000, or if you have more than $600,000 in savings.

When grandparents make such a gift, however, it can have income tax repercussions for the child's parents. For whatever reason, the Internal Revenue Service has at times ruled that when a parent is under an obligation by law to support the children and the grandparents cover the cost, it is considered to be a payment that is taxable to the parent. You'll want to consult your accountant about the rules on this depending on your unique circumstances.

## CHARITABLE GIFTS

If you want to boost your current income while lowering eventual estate taxes, then you should consider making a charitable gift. There are many estate planning techniques that can lower estate taxes, bolster your current income, and help out a charity you believe in. There are no limits by the Internal Revenue Service on the amount you can contribute to a charity in any given year. A gift to charity is a deduction on your income tax return. The deduction may be limited to 20 or 30 percent, but could be as high as 50 percent of your adjusted gross income each year, provided you have the proper receipts. It will depend on the type of property and organization to which it is given.

To comply with IRS regulations, when you give a gift, you must have a receipt from the charity and documentation that describes your donation and its current value.

# CHARITABLE REMAINDER TRUSTS

These trusts allow you to give to a charity at a set future date, take the tax deduction (not the entire amount), but still receive the income from the assets while you are alive. You'll need an attorney to set up this type of trust. The process lets you give stocks or a sum of money to the trust and then take a tax deduction for the gift. The amount you can deduct depends on your age, the value of the property or asset you gave to the charity, and how much of the payout from the income you hold on to.

 **Charitable Remainder Trust**   A charitable remainder trust lets you give to a charity at a future date and get tax benefits now.

All the income from your asset continues to flow directly back to you either immediately or after you retire. You can wait as long as you want to start accepting income from the trust. Sometimes it's better to wait until after you retire to enjoy the benefits. And there's no capital gains tax if the appreciated assets are sold and the money reinvested in income-generating assets such as bonds. But you can't take the asset back, so you absolutely shouldn't consider putting all your assets in a charitable remainder trust.

The charity gets all the assets when you die or on the date you set. By giving the gift this way, you have taken the assets out of your estate and have eliminated estate taxes on them. The

best assets to earmark for this type of charitable gift are those investments that have appreciated substantially over the years, like stocks or real estate holdings.

 **Charitable Gift Annuities**   This is another way to hand over assets that have appreciated substantially, say, a piece of land that you paid $200,000 for a decade ago that is now worth closer to $700,000. This annuity allows you to give property, cash, or other investments to a charity. In return, you get a guaranteed fixed sum of income from that asset for the rest of your life.

## How a Charitable Gift Annuity Works

The charity sells your donation and uses the proceeds to buy an annuity. You, then, get a tax deduction equal to what the charity can sell your asset for. The biggest drawback is that you are forced to accept a fixed sum of income from the annuity that the charity purchases. Over time, inflation can erode that payout to you substantially.

This type of estate planning can be tricky, so you'll definitely want to consult your attorney about the details.

In this lesson, you learned estate planning strategies that can help reduce your tax burden in your retirement years and pass along your assets after you die. In the next lesson, you'll learn how to get professional financial guidance to help get your overall retirement plan in place.

# 19

# CHOOSING A FINANCIAL PLANNER

*In this lesson, you'll learn how to hire someone to help you develop your retirement plan.*

## CAN YOU DO IT YOURSELF?

There's no reason why you can't handle your own retirement planning, but it does take time and patience. As a result, you may want to turn to a full-time financial planner to do the legwork. You should be aware that professional advice and homework comes at a price. Even a basic plan could run you from $500 to $1,000. Remember, these fees might otherwise be funneled into one of your retirement accounts.

When a catastrophe strikes, it's often hard to make clear financial decisions. And if you are widowed, you may have a lump-sum insurance payout to invest, or in the case of a divorce, a cash settlement of some type. Moreover, everyone from unscrupulous brokers to concerned relatives will be offering you advice on where to invest your money. This is a time to go slowly, and a good financial planner can help you sort things out without making any rash decisions.

If you opt to hire a planner, don't forget it's still your responsibility to approve the investment choices. You can't just throw up your hands and say "Just do what you think is best." Moreover, you might want to hire someone to just help you devise a strategy, or put together a road map. Then you take over the actual investing job, saving yourself those additional fees a planner might tack on.

# How to Choose a Planner

The financial planning industry is a quagmire and for the most part, it is unregulated. Anyone can call themselves a financial planner. One important credential a planner should have is a "CFP," meaning "Certified Financial Planner."

**Certified Financial Planner (CFP)**    A CFP means that someone has undertaken an intense series of courses and exams, plus 15 hours of continuing education annually. The CFP is granted by the College of Financial Planning, a nonprofit industry educational arm.

Many CFPs as well as other planners earn a portion of their income from commissions on financial products they sell to you. This is a conflict of interest you want to avoid. It's up to you to find out how they operate. For the same reason, you should probably avoid insurance agents and stockbrokers who boast of being financial advisors.

The best financial planners are usually "fee-only" planners. There are about 4,000 of these planners in the country.

**Fee-Only**   Fee-only planners earn no commissions on what you buy. The planners simply charge a fee that they set upfront, either by the hour, the planning session, or based on a percentage of your portfolio.

There are still other planners who are a type of hybrid called "fee and commission" who usually charge a flat fee as well as earn commissions on some of the investments they recommend to you.

## FINDING A PLANNER

There are plenty of good places to help you find a financial planner to suit your needs. You might start by asking friends and relatives for recommendations. There are also several organizations that provide lists of planners in your area who have passed certified courses in investment planning:

- The Institute of Certified Financial Planners (800-282-7526) maintains a database of more than 7,000 planners and will send you information about planners in your area that have passed a course and received a CFP.

- The International Association for Financial Planning (IAFP) (800-945-4237) will send you a list of five members who are doing business in your area. They also include a free guide called *Consumer Guide to Comprehensive Financial Planning* that provides details on your rights as a customer. Their list is made up of planners who have practiced for at least three years and have submitted references from six clients.

- The National Association of Personal Financial Advisors (800-366-2732) is an association of fee-only planners that can send you a list of planners in your area.

- You can check with the Securities and Exchange Commission information line (202-942-8088) or the National Association of Securities Dealers (800-289-9999) to be certain a planner is registered as "someone who gives advice about securities for compensation" and check if any complaints have been filed against the planner. The SEC won't recommend any advisors, but it can tell you if there is any pending enforcement action against the planner or her firm.

The best way to find a planner is to ask for referrals from other professionals you work with such as attorneys, accountants, or insurance agents. The type of advisor you need will depend on how much help you want and how savvy you are about investing.

# What You Should Ask a Planner

Take the time to interview a potential planner to find out if that person is right for you. Here are some questions that you should ask:

- What is the firm's background and area of expertise?
- How long have you been a planner?
- How long have you been at this firm?
- What is your educational background?

- Are you full-time or part-time?
- Are you a member of a professional planning organization?
- Do you take continuing education courses each year?
- What kind of clients do you have?
- Do you have many women clients?
- What is the average size of the portfolios you manage?
- Do you have a special investment strategy?
- What retirement services do you provide?
- Are you bonded?
- Will we have a written contract?
- How are you compensated?
- Are you registered with the SEC?
- Can you give me three references?
- What has been your best investment of the last few years?
- What is your biggest investment mistake of the last few years?

## WHAT A PLANNER SHOULD ASK YOU

A reputable planner should also be interested in your unique situation. To get a feel for what your needs will be, he or she should take the time to ask you several important questions. Here's what you should be prepared to answer:

- What are your assets?

- What are your liabilities?

- What are your monthly housing costs and other expenditures?

- What are your future goals?

- What is your income?

- What benefits does your company offer?

- Do you have an estate plan?

- Are you married?

- Do you have children or other dependents?

- What insurance coverage, including health, life, disability, and property, do you currently have?

- What is your money philosophy?

- How much money management do you want to do yourself?

- Do you expect to inherit money?

- How secure is your current job?

- Will you have to support your husband one day?

- How risk-tolerant are you when it comes to investing?

Trust your instincts. Don't choose a planner unless you feel comfortable with the person. It's your money. Your planner doesn't have to be your best buddy, but you should have a relaxed rapport and trust him or her.

In this lesson, you learned how to find a financial planner to help you develop your retirement plan. In the next lesson, you'll learn about sources of retirement planning advice that you can tap into via your home computer.

# GOING ON-LINE FOR HELP

## 20

*In this lesson, you'll learn how to find useful retirement planning and investing information using your personal computer and modem.*

## ON-LINE SERVICES

One of the simplest ways to learn about investing for retirement and keep track of your current portfolio is to subscribe to an on-line service—America Online, CompuServe, or Prodigy. The basic cost is $9.95 a month for five hours on-line and $2.95 per additional hour. You may have to pay extra for some of the services, especially on CompuServe. On all three services you can do the following:

- Receive stock and mutual fund share price quotes (delayed by 15 minutes)

- Learn the latest financial market news

- Read financial publications

- Download in-depth profiles of thousands of mutual funds and publicly traded companies

- Set up accounts with brokerages to trade via your computer

- Talk with other cyber investors

# INVESTMENT FORUMS

All three on-line services have chat rooms for personal investors. In these chat rooms people exchange ideas, tout investments, and grouse about bad investments. Two reputable sites for investors are the Motley Fool (Keyword: *FOOL*) on America Online and the American Association of Individual Investors (Keyword: *AAII*) site located on both CompuServe and AOL.

 Be skeptical, though, because there can be shady operators in these rooms who will try to con you into buying a bogus investment. Their goal is to pump up the share price, so they can sell at a profit. When the stock price falls, you get left holding the bag. It's foolish to buy on any of these tips; always do your own careful research.

# AMERICA ONLINE

The offerings on America Online are plentiful for beginning investors in particular. You have access to Morningstar's comprehensive database (Keyword: *Morningstar*) of 6,500 mutual fund profiles and 6,000 public company reports. You can pull up a company's earnings estimate by clicking the icon in the personal investing section for First Call (Keyword: *FirstCall*). First Call is a group that compiles analyst predictions from well-respected firms such as Alex Brown & Sons Inc., Brown Brothers Harriman & Co., and Dean Witter Reynolds, Inc.

There's a Wall Street dictionary if you are stumped by an unfamiliar investment term. You can access Hoover's Handbook (Keyword: *Hoover*) of 1,000 large company profiles. You can get a firm's annual 10-k report on file with the Securities and Exchange Commission (Keyword: *Edgar*), which includes share price histories and audited financial records provided via Disclosure Inc. (Keyword: *Disclosure*).

Moreover, both Fidelity (Keyword: *Fidelity*) and Vanguard (Keyword: *Vanguard*) offer Investor Centers that let you view detailed descriptions of their funds, including annual returns as compared to the S & P 500, Lipper analytical ratings, fee and expense data, and bios of the managers. The sites for Fidelity and Vanguard also feature interactive worksheets to help you calculate how much you need to save for retirement and help you determine your individual risk tolerance. The sites also help you determine what the proper asset allocation mix is for your risk profile and years away from retirement, as well as provide you with a list of their funds that best fit your needs.

If you want to invest on-line, you can open a brokerage account with PC Financial Network, a division of Donaldson, Lufkin & Jenrette (Keyword: *PCFN*). You will be charged commissions for any trading you do. For example, $1,000 invested in shares of a company would cost $40.

# CompuServe

This is a great service for mutual fund information. Moreover, experienced investors will find more extensive data here. There are additional costs, however, to access those resources, such as $1 to get a company report from S & P or five cents for a historical stock price quote. You can tap into FundWatch Online (to access, type Go:FundWatch), provided by *Money Magazine*, which allows you to screen through over 4,500 mutual funds using your own investment criteria, including risk and performance ratings and asset allocations. Extensive research material, such as Disclosure Inc. (Go:Disclosure) filings, Standard & Poor's reports, and Dun & Bradstreet information is available for additional fees (Go:Stocks).

You can place trades via an account opened with one of three brokerages: E*Trade Securities (Go:ETrade), Max Ule, and Quick & Reilly. With both E*Trade and Max Ule, you pay only commissions on trades. Quick & Reilly charges an extra $14 per connect hour during the day and $4 per hour in the evening.

# PRODIGY

This is the best organized of the three services, but it lacks the resources of the other two. You can pull up "Stocks at a Glance" or "Funds at a Glance" to get the most recent share price, past performance, and latest Dow Jones clippings. For $1.95 a day, you can use "Stock Hunter" to screen 6,000 stocks based on criteria you request, such as yield, p/e ratio, or 5-year return on equity. Mutual fund companies Dreyfus, Fidelity, and Scudder all have sites to provide information on their funds and advice on retirement planning. You can open an account with PC Financial Network.

# THE INTERNET'S WORLD WIDE WEB

You can access the Internet through one of the on-line services, which now provide Web browsers, or you can explore via an Internet service provider, which for a monthly fee of about $20 provides a direct link to the Web. The pace of new offerings cropping up on the Web for people looking for financial information is astounding. For mutual funds alone, there are more than 60 companies that have set up home pages in the last year. Dozens more are on the way, as the SEC ruled last year that distributing prospectuses and annual reports electronically is acceptable.

## Where to Start

A good place to start is with a search service such as Yahoo (http://www.yahoo.com). Click the "Business and Economy" section. Next click "Investments," and you're on your way. This search engine will link you to most mutual fund company home pages, financial magazines, and the SEC's Edgar database (http://www.sec.gov.com), where you can view any stock or mutual fund filing.

## Other Useful Sites

- Networth Investor Network (http://www.Networth. galt.com), is a kind of cybermall for investors. You'll find Morningstar reports and direct links to fund home pages, stock and bond quotes, and much more.

- Investorama (http://www.investorama.com) is another site loaded with links to financial Web sites.

- The on-line site of *Mutual Funds* magazine (http:// www.mfmag.com), the publication edited by *Mutual Fund Forecaster and Fundwatch* newsletter publisher

Norm Fosback, serves up all the magazine's articles, plus access to a database of 7,000 funds and links to homepages.

Among the best fund family sites:

- The Calvert Group (http://www.calvertgroup.com)
- Fidelity (http://www.fid-inv.com)
- Gabelli (http://www.gabelli.com)
- T.Rowe Price (http://www.troweprice.com)
- Vanguard (http://www.vanguard.com)

What the fund pages offer:

You'll find investment advice such as libraries that define different types of mutual funds and their investment goals, worksheets that calculate your risk tolerance, and interactive retirement planning and college saving worksheets that help you calculate how much you will need to save each year to meet those goals. The sites can also help select an investment strategy based on your individual objectives and time horizon, deliver detailed reports on their funds, daily updates of shareholder account values, a list of recent transactions for shareholders, and downloadable prospectuses.

In this lesson, you learned how to use your computer to make your retirement planning easier. This is the final lesson in *The 10 Minute Guide to Retirement for Women.* You now know enough to start stitching together a cohesive retirement plan. Facing the financial challenges of retirement takes determination, hard work, and some sacrifices along the way. Compared to the alternative—winding up with too little, too late—you'll find the task well worth the effort.

# RESOURCES

Here are some useful resources and phone
numbers to help you with your retirement planning research.

## CREDIT REPORTS

TRW: 800-422-4879

Trans Union: 601-939-0446

Equifax: 770-612-2500

## INSURANCE

Insurance Information Institute: 800-331-9146

Quotesmith: 800-556-9393

## OVERALL

American Association of Retired Persons: 202-434-3525

National Council on Aging: 202-479-1200

National Center for Women and Retirement Research:
800-426-7386

Social Security Administration: 800-772-1213

U.S. Department of Labor: 202-219-8776

## Mutual Funds

Morningstar Mutual Funds Rating Service: 800-876-5005

CDA Wiesenberger Mutual Funds: 800-232-2285

Value Line: 800-825-8354

## Investment Clubs

American Association of Individual Investors: 312-280-0170

National Association of Investment Clubs: 810-583-6242

## Financial Planners and Brokers

Certified Financial Planner Board of Standards: 888-237-6275

National Association of Securities Dealers: 800-289-9999

National Association of Insurance Commissioners: 816-842-3600

North American Securities Administration Association: 202-737-0900

Securities and Exchange Commission: 800-732-0330

Institute of Certified Financial Planners: 800-282-7526

The International Association for Financial Planning: 800-945-4237

The National Association of Personal Financial Advisors: 800-366-2732

## Treasury Bonds

The Bureau of Public Debt: 202-874-4000

## Rating Services

A.M. Best: 908-439-2200

Moody's Investors Service: 212-553-0377

Standard & Poor's: 212-208-1527

Weiss Research: 800-289-9222

## Annuities

Fee for Service Annuity Brokerage: 800-874-5662

Fidelity: 800-634-9361

T. Rowe Price: 800-469-6587

Charles Schwab: 800-838-0650

Vanguard: 800-522-5555

## Working After Retirement

Senior Career Planning and Placement Service: 212-529-6660

Operation ABLE: 312-782-3335

## Housing

U.S. Housing and Urban Development Office: 800-669-9777

# GLOSSARY

**401(k)**  A company's retirement benefit plan that lets you, the employee, make regular, tax-deferred contributions from your salary each pay period. Frequently the firm will match a percentage of your contribution.

**403(b) plan**  Similar to a 401(k), but set up for public employees and employees of non-profit organizations.

**Accrued benefits**  All retirement benefits you have earned to date from an employer.

**Adjusted gross income**  Your total income minus all IRA or Keogh contributions or business expenses.

**Aggressive growth fund**  These funds generally invest in small cutting-edge companies in industries such as high-tech.

**American Depository Receipts (ADR)**  Roughly 1,300 foreign companies now trade on the U.S. stock exchanges in the form of ADRs, dollar-denominated securities that represent a given number of company shares.

**Annuity**  A type of investment in which you, a policyholder, make either installment or lump-sum payments to an insurance company and in turn get money at retirement for a period of time or for life. The money grows tax-free until it is withdrawn.

**Asset allocation**  Your investment mix spread among stocks, bonds, mutual funds, etc.

**Balanced fund**   A mutual fund that invests in both growth and income stocks and bonds.

**Blue-chip stocks**   The shares of a stable, well-known company that has a reputation for regular earnings and dividends.

**Bond**   A debt of the government or a corporation. The buyer provides money to the institution, then it agrees to pay the sum back with interest at specific times.

**Capital gain or loss**   What you make or lose from selling an asset such as a home or stocks.

**Certificate of deposit (CD)**   A deposit in a bank for a set time period with a guaranteed interest rate. There is usually a penalty for an early withdrawal.

**Common stock**   An equity interest in a public company.

**Compounded interest**   Interest added to your principal plus the interest that has been previously earned.

**Cyclical stocks**   Shares of companies whose earnings rise and fall with the economy, such as automobile makers and housing firms.

**Defined benefit plan**   A traditional pension plan where your employer devises a formula based on your salary and number of years with the company for calculating income to be paid to you when you retire. At that time, the money is paid out to you on a regular monthly basis for the rest of your life.

**Defined contribution plan**   A plan in which your employer contributes a set amount for you annually to a retirement fund. When you retire, you are usually paid the accumulated funds in a lump sum.

**Dividend**   A payout by a company of a certain part of its earnings in the form of cash or stock to shareholders.

**Dollar cost averaging**   Buying shares in stocks and mutual funds at timed intervals using the same amount of money each time.

**Dow Jones Average**   This is a calculation that averages the daily stock prices of 30 U.S. blue-chip stocks and is used as a way to track the rise and fall of the stock market as a whole.

**Employee Stock Ownership Plan (ESOP)**   A plan in which your employer offers a retirement plan with contributions in the form of the company's stock.

**Fund family**   Mutual funds that are run by the same investment company, such as Fidelity or Vanguard.

**Government bond**   A Savings bond, Treasury bill, Treasury bond, or Treasury note sold by the U.S. government.

**Growth fund**   The aim of these funds is long-term appreciation. They generally invest in well-established companies.

**Guaranteed-Income Contract (GIC)**   A fixed-interest investment, usually earning no more than 5 percent, issued by an insurance company that can last as long as seven years.

**Income fund**   A mutual fund that invests primarily for income and dividends.

**Index fund**   A mutual fund that models itself after a particular stock index, such as the S & P 500.

**Individual Retirement Account (IRA)**   This is a tax-deferred type of pension account that lets you invest up to $2,000 annually ($2,500 if your spouse is not employed) in a special account and not pay tax on what accumulates until the money is withdrawn at retirement. You pay a penalty if you withdraw the funds before age 59½, and distributions must begin by age 70½.

**International funds**   These funds invest in stocks of non-U.S. companies. Some funds specialize in companies from a single country or region.

**Investment club**   A group of people who meet to research and buy stocks as one entity.

**Junk bond**   A bond that is issued by a corporation that has a high risk of defaulting. Since they are considered to be risky investments, they pay out a high percentage of interest.

**Keogh plan**   This is a tax-deferred retirement plan for people who are self-employed. Up to 25 percent of your income can be put in a Keogh.

**Liquidity**   How fast you can get your money back from an investment with its earnings.

**Load**   This is the commission charged by some mutual funds when you buy or sell shares. No-load funds charge no upfront commissions. All funds charge annual management fees, usually .5 to 1.5 percent a year.

**Money-market account**   A bank savings account that typically pays higher interest than a regular savings account.

**Municipal bond**   A bond sold in denominations of $1,000 and $5,000 that is issued by a local or state government. It pays interest that is exempt from federal and usually state and local tax as well.

**Mutual fund**   A group that pools the funds of many people and invests in securities.

**Net asset value**   The value of a mutual fund's portfolio that adds up the prices of all the securities in the fund, minus any liabilities, and divides that sum by the number of outstanding shares.

**Net worth**   Your assets minus your liabilities.

**Pension**   Payments made by an employer to a former employee upon retirement.

**Portfolio**   This is how people refer to all of their various investments and usually includes several types of mutual funds, individual stocks, bonds, and real estate holdings.

**Price-earnings ratio**   The current stock price divided by a company's earnings per share.

**Prospectus**   This is a document that gives you background information about a mutual fund or a company, including historical financial performance.

**Qualified domestic relations order**   This is a state domestic relations court order that requires by law an employee's retirement plan to be divided between the employee, a spouse, and any children in case of a divorce.

**Rate of return**   How much will your money earn in a given investment over a set time period.

**Rating**   A score given by independent firms such as Moody's or Standard & Poor's that gauges the financial strength of a bond.

**Reverse mortgage**   This is a type of mortgage in which the lender pays you, providing you, the homeowner, are over age 62, a monthly sum for a set term of years based on the total equity in the house. When you sell your house, or die, the lender is repaid from the proceeds of the sale.

**Rollover IRA**   This is a process where you move the assets from one qualified retirement plan to another one. You must have your ex-employer do this within 60 days of you leaving the company, or you might face a tax penalty.

**Safety**   This is one way of measuring whether or not you will lose money in a particular investment.

**SEC**   The Securities and Exchange Commission is the federal government's agency in charge of regulating the securities industry and enforcing any laws.

**Sector funds**   The fund's aim is to invest solely in one single industry, say, auto stocks.

**Simplified Employee Pension Plan (SEP)**   This is a retirement plan for anyone who is self-employed. An IRA is set up and a percentage of earnings, up to 13 percent of your net earnings, is contributed tax-deferred until you retire.

**Social Security**   Retirement benefits that are paid to you by the federal government provided you have been a wage earner for 40 quarters. A sum of $2,280 earned in a year equals four quarters of coverage.

**Socially conscious funds**   These funds invest in firms that have an excellent environmental record or that don't make or sell politically incorrect goods.

**Term life insurance**   Life insurance in which the benefit is paid only upon the death of the insured person.

**Treasury bill**   A short-term debt instrument issued by the federal government. These bills mature in periods of three months, six months, or one year. The minimum purchase is $10,000.

**Treasury bond**    A long-term debt instrument issued by the federal government that matures in ten to 30 years. These bonds are sold in denominations of $1,000 and pay interest every six months.

**Treasury note**    A medium-term debt instrument issued by the federal government that matures in one to ten years. The minimum purchase is $5,000 for under four years; for over four years it's $1,000. Interest is paid every six months.

**Universal life insurance**    This is a type of life insurance where a portion of the premium goes toward the purchase of insurance and the rest is invested.

**Vesting**    Employers who offer a 401(k) plan usually contribute some amount to the plan on a partially matching basis after a certain number of employment years known as a vesting period. A vesting period is usually around five years.

**Zero coupon bond**    A bond that sells at a deep discount from the face value and pays no interest until maturity, when it is redeemable at the full face value.

# INDEX

## SYMBOLS

1035(a) form (IRS Tax Code), 44
401(k) plans, 9
    GICs (Guaranteed Investment
      Contracts), 46-48
    petitioning for spouse's, 69
    rollovers, 13

## A

accessing the Internet, 117-118
age
    allocating investments, 23
    balancing portfolios, 56-59
aggressive growth mutual
  funds, 36
A.M. Best telephone number,
  77, 122
America Online, investments, 115
American Association for
  Retired Persons, 74, 120
American Association of
  Individual Investors in
  Chicago, 54, 115, 121
American Stock Exchange, 29
annuities, 41-43
    charitable gifts, 107
    deferred, 44
    immediate, 44
    insurance companies, 43
    retirement planning
      research, 122
    surrender fees, 42
    withdrawing, 44-45
applying for Social Security,
  81-82
assets, 5
    allocation, 56-59
    giving away, 106-107
    living trusts, 100-103
    prenuptial agreements, 68

## B

balanced mutual funds, 36
BICs (bank investment
  contracts), 49
Blue-chip stocks, 32
bond mutual funds, 38
bonds, 23-25
    Corporate, 25
    defined, 24
    Municipal, 25
    purchasing, 24
    treasury, 121
    U.S. Treasuries, 24
    Zero coupon, 25
borrowing money
    from home equity, 85-86
    from reverse mortgages, 86-89
break in service, 64
brokerage firms, discount, 53
brokers, 53
    discount, 31
    purchasing bonds, 24
    resources for retirement
      planning research, 121
Bureau of Public Debt, 24, 121
businesses, starting, 83-84
buying, see purchasing

## C

Calvert Group, 119
cash-value life insurance, 94-98
CDA Wiesenberger Mutual
  Funds, 121
CDs (certificates of deposit), 26
CFPs (Certified Financial
  Planners), 109, 121
charitable gifts, 105-107
charitable remainder trusts,
  106-107

Charles Schwab, 31, 122
choosing, *see* selecting
clubs, investment, 54
commissions, 52-54
companies
    finances, 33-34
    insurance annuities, 43
    small, mutual funds, 36
compounding, defined, 21
CompuServe investments, 116
Consumer Affairs Section, 89
Corporate bonds, 25
costs, *see* fees
credit reports, 120

# D

deferred annuities, 44
defined benefit plans, 8
defined contribution plans,
    *see* 401(k) plans
disability insurance, 98-99
Disclosure Inc., 116
discount brokerage firms, 53
discount brokers, 31
diversification, 32
    ESOPs (Employee Stock
        Ownership Plans), 50
    GICs (Guaranteed Investment
        Contracts), 47-48
dividends, investments, 30
divorce
    effect on savings, 67-68
    prenuptial agreements, 68
    timing, 70
donating money, *see* charitable
    gifts
DRIPs (dividend reinvestment
    programs), 52
Duff & Phelps, 77

# E

E*Trade Securities, 117
early retirement, 79-80
education
    gifts, 104-105
    investments, 54
Employee Stock Ownership
    Plans (ESOPs), *see* ESOPs
employers
    early retirement offers, 79-80
    pension plans, 8-9

Equifax, 120
ESOPs (Employee Stock
    Ownership Plans), 9, 46, 49-50
    defined, 49
    diversification, 50
    problems, 50
estate planning, 100-103
estimating future living
    expenses, 14-20
Evergreen Enterprises, 52
expenses
    defined, 4
    health care, 71, 74-78
    retirement, 14, 16-20

# F

Fabulous Places to Retire in
    America, 90
Family and Medical Leave Act, 65
Fannie Mae's "Homekeeper," 89
Federal Housing Authority
    (FHA), 87
Fee for Service Annuity
    Brokerage, 43, 122
fee-only financial planners, 110
fees
    annuities, 42
    long-term healthcare, 76-78
    Medicare, 71-73
    online services, 114
    purchasing stocks, 31
    surrender, 42
FHA (Federal Housing
    Authority), 87
Fidelity Investments, 53, 116,
    119, 122
finances
    assets, *see* assets
    companies, 33-34
    income, *see* income
    liabilities, *see* liabilities
    retirement income, 1-4, 8,
        11-20
financial planners, 108-109
    Certified Financial Planners
        (CFPs), 109
    fee-only, 110
    finding, 109-113
    resources for retirement
        planning research, 121
finding
    financial planners, 109-113

long-term health care policies,
76-77
Medicare information, 74
part-time work, 83
reverse mortgage information, 89
stock information, 33
First Call, 115
foreign stocks, 33
forums, investments, 115
freelancing, Keogh plans, 10
Funds at a Glance, 117
FundWatch Online, 117

## G

Gabelli Web site, 119
GICs (Guaranteed Investment
Contracts), 46
defined, 46-49
diversification, 47
problems, 48-49
gifts
charitable, 105-107
educational, 104-105
medical, 104-105
global mutual funds, 37
growth and income mutual
funds, 37
Guaranteed Investment
Contracts (GICs), *see* GICs

## H

health care, 71
long-term care, 74-78
Medicare, 71-74
Health Insurance Association of
America, 76
*Hoover's Handbook*, 116
Household Bank's Household
program, 89
housing
equity loans, 85-86
renting for income, 90
resources for retirement
planning research, 122
selling, 89-90

## I

immediate annuities, 44
income
defined, 4
inflation's effect, 2

preretirement, matching, 1
renting homes for, 90
retirement, 14-20
social security, 11-13
sources of, 8
income mutual funds, 37
income stocks, 32
index mutual funds, 37
Individual Retirement
Accounts (IRAs), *see* IRAs
inflation, effect on income, 2
Institute of Certified Financial
Planners, 110, 121
insurance
companies, 43
disability, 98-99
life, 91-93
calculating amount needed, 93
cash-value, 94-98
purchasing, 93-98
quote services, 97
term insurance, 94, 96
withdrawing money from, 95
long-term care, 74-75
cost, 76
cost cutting, 78
coverage, 75
finding policies, 76-77
Medicare, 71-74
resources for retirement
planning research, 120
Insurance Information
Institute (III), 120
Insurance Quote Services
Inc., 97
International Association for
Financial Planning, 110, 121
international mutual funds, 37
Internet, accessing the, 117-118
investment clubs, 121
investments
allocating via age, 23
annuities, 41-45
balancing portfolios, 56-59
BICs (bank investment
contracts), 49
bonds, 23-25
brokers, 53
discount, 31
purchasing bonds, 24
resources for retirement
planning research, 121
CDs (certificates of deposit), 26
clubs, 54

commissions, 52-54
comparison of annual returns, 30
compounding, 21
diversification, 32
dividends, 30
education, 54
ESOPs (Employee Stock
    Ownership Plans), *see* ESOPs
GICs (Guaranteed
    Investment Contracts),
    *see* GICs
money market accounts, 26
mutual funds, *see* mutual funds
on-line services, 114-118
risky investments, 21-23, 51-52
stocks, *see* stocks
Investorama, 118
IRAs (Individual Retirement
    Accounts), 10
irrevocable trusts, 102
IRS Tax Code 1035(a) form, 44

## J-K

Jack White & Co., telephone
    number, 53
jobs
    break in service, 64-65
    changing, 61-63
    part-time work, 83
    rollover accounts, 13
    time off, effect on savings, 63-65
    working after retirement, 80
    *see also* working
joint-and-survivor annuity
    withdrawals, 45

Keogh plans, 10

## L

liabilities
    defined, 4-6
    prenuptial agreements, 68
life annuity withdrawals, 45
life insurance, 91-93
    calculating, 93
    cash-value, 94-98
    purchasing, 93-94
        *cash-value policies*, 95, 97-98
        *quote services*, 97
        *term policies*, 96
    term insurance, 94, 96

withdrawing money from, 95
living expenses, future, 14, 16-20
living trusts, 100-103
loans, home equity, 85-86
long-term growth mutual
    funds, 37
long-term health care, 74-75
    cost, 76
    cost cutting, 78
    coverage, 75
    finding policies, 76-77
loss of spouse, effect on savings,
    66-67
low-load insurers, 43

## M

marriage, prenuptial
    agreements, 68
marital trusts, 101-102
medical expenses, 71
    long-term care, 74-75
        *cost*, 76, 78
        *coverage*, 75
        *finding policies*, 76-77
    Medicare, 71-73
        *resources for finding
            information on*, 74
        *supplement policies*, 73-74
medical gifts, 104-105
Medicare, 71-73
    resources for finding
        information on, 74
    supplement policies, 73-74
Medigap policies, 73-74
money
    borrowing
        *from home equity*, 85-86
        *from reverse mortgages*,
            86-89
    retirement needs, 1-4, 14-15
    saving, *see* saving
    withdrawing from life
        insurance, 95
money market accounts, 26
money market mutual funds, 38
Moody's Investors Service,
    77, 122
Morningstar Mutual Funds
    Rating Service, 121
mortgages, reverse, 86-89
Motley Fool, 115
Municipal bonds, 25

mutual funds, 35
  aggressive growth, 36
  balanced, 36
  bond, 38
  defined, 35-36
  global, 37
  growth and income, 37
  index, 37
  international, 37
  long-term growth, 37
  money market, 38
  performance, 39
  purchasing, 40
  resources for retirement
    planning research, 121
  sector, 38
  selecting, 36-39
  socially-conscious, 38
*Mutual Funds* magazine, 118

## N

NASDAQ (National Association
  of Securities Dealers
  Automated Quotation
  system), 29, 111, 121
National Association of Insur-
  ance Commissioners, 76, 121
National Association of
  Investment Clubs, , 121
National Association of
  Investors Corp., 31, 55
National Association of Personal
  Financial Advisors, 111, 121
National Association of
  Securities Dealers Automated
  Quotation system (NASDAQ),
  29, 111, 121
National Center for Home
  Equity Conversion, 89
National Center for Women
  and Retirement Research, 120
National Council on Aging, 120
Networth Investor Network, 118
New York Stock Exchange, 29
no-load stocks, 31
North American Securities
  Administration Association, 121

## O-P

on-line services, investments,
  114-115

America Online, 115-116
CompuServe, 116-117
forums, 115
Prodigy, 117
World Wide Web, 117-118
Operation ABLE, 122

part-time work, 83
partial retirement, 82
  finding part-time work, 83
  starting a business, 83-84
PC Financial Network, 116
pension plans, 8-9
performance of mutual funds, 39
petitioning for spouse's 401(k)
  plans, 69
plans, retirement
  financial planners, 108-113
  loss of spouse, 67
  pensions, 8-9
  self-employment, 7
  types, 7-11
  vesting periods, 13
portfolios, balancing, 56-59
preretirement income,
  matching, 1
prenuptial agreements, 68
problems
  ESOPs (Employee Stock
    Ownership Plans), 50
  GICs (Guaranteed Investment
    Contracts), 48-49
Prodigy, 117
prospectuses, 53
purchasing
  bonds, 24
  life insurance, 93-98
  mutual funds, 40
  stocks, 31-33

## Q-R

QDRO (Qualified Domestic
  Relations Order), 69-70
Quick & Reilly, 31, 53
quote services, life insurance, 97
Quotesmith Corp., 97, 120

rating services, 122
renting homes for income, 90
resources
  financial planners, 110-111
  long-term health care policies, 76
  Medicare, 74

retirement planning research, 120-122
reverse mortgages, 89
retirement
early, 79-80
income, *see* income
partial, 82
*finding part-time work, 83*
*starting a business, 83-84*
plans
*financial planners, 108-113*
*loss of spouse, 67*
*pensions, 8-9*
*self-employment, 7*
*types, 7-11*
*vesting periods, 13*
preretirement income, 1
working after, 80-81, 122
reverse mortgages, 86-89
disadvantages, 88
resources for finding information, 89
structure, 87
risky investments, 21-23, 51-52
rollover accounts, 13

## S

safe investments, 21-23
salaries, inflation's effect on, 2
saving
inflation's effect on, 2
investments, *see* investments
job changing, effect on, 61-63
loss of spouse, effect on, 66-67
retirement needs, 16-20
SCORE (Service Corps of Retired Executives), 84
sector mutual funds, 38
Securities and Exchange Commission, 111, 116, 121
selecting
annuities, 43
financial planners, 109-113
life insurance, 93-98
mutual funds, 36-39
trustees, 102-103
SelectQuote, 97
self-employment
Keogh plans, 10
retirement plans, 7
selling homes, 89-90
Senior Career Planning & Placement Service, 83, 122

SEPs (Simplified Employee Pension Plans), 11
Service Corps of Retired Executives (SCORE), 84
Simplified Employee Pension Plans (SEPs), 11
sites (Web), *see* Web sites
small companies
mutual funds, 36
stocks, 32
Social Security
benefits, 11-13
increasing payments, 81-82
working, 84
Social Security Administration, 74, 120
socially-conscious mutual funds, 38
spouses
loss of, effect on retirement savings, 66-67
petitioning for 401(k) plans, 69
Standard & Poor's stock reports, 34, 77, 122
starting
businesses, 83
investment clubs, 55
stock dividend reinvestment programs, *see* DRIPs (dividend reinvestment programs)
Stock Hunter, 117
stocks
Blue-chip, 32
defined, 28-30
exchanges, 28-29
finding company information on, 33-34
foreign, 33
income, 32
no-load, 31
purchasing, 31-33
small-company, 32
Stocks at a Glance, 117
surrender fees, 42
systematic annuity withdrawals, 45

## T

T. Rowe Price, 119, 122
term insurance, 94, 96
TermQuote, 97

Trans Union, 120
TransAmerica Corp.'s Home First
    plan, 89
treasury bonds, 121
Treasury Direct, 24
trustees, selecting, 102-103
trusts
    charitable remainder, 106-107
    living, 100-103

## U-V

U.S. Department of Labor, 9, 120
U.S. Housing and Urban
    Development Office, 122
U.S. Treasuries, 24

Value Line Investment
    Survey, 34
Vanguard, 116, 119, 122
vesting periods, 13

## W

Wall Street dictionary, 116
Web sites
    American Association of
        Individual Investors, 115
    Calvert Group, 119
    Disclosure Inc., 116
    E*Trade Securities, 117
    Fidelity, 116, 119
    First Call, 115
    FundWatch Online, 117
    Gabelli, 119
    Hoover's Handbook, 116
    Investorama, 118
    Motley Fool, 115
    Mutual Funds magazine, 118

Networth Investor Network, 118
PC Financial Network, 116
Securities and Exchange
    Commission, 116
T. Rowe Price, 119
Vanguard, 116, 119, 122
Yahoo, 118
Weiss Research, 77, 122
withdrawing
    annuities, 44-45
    money from life insurance, 95
working
    after retirement, 80, 122
    part-time, 83
    Social Security, 84
    see also jobs
World Wide Web (WWW)
    investments, 117
    sites, see Web sites

## X-Z

Yahoo, 118

Zero coupon bonds, 25